The Incomplete, True, Authentic, and Wonderful History of May Day

T0163860

Editor: Sasha Lilley

Spectre is a series of penetrating and indispensable works of, and about, radical political economy. Spectre lays bare the dark underbelly of politics and economics, publishing outstanding and contrarian perspectives on the maelstrom of capital—and emancipatory alternatives—in crisis. The companion Spectre Classics imprint unearths essential works of radical history, political economy, theory and practice, to illuminate the present with brilliant, yet unjustly neglected, ideas from the past.

Spectre

Greg Albo, Sam Gindin, and Leo Panitch, *In and Out of Crisis: The Global Financial Meltdown and Left Alternatives*

David McNally, *Global Slump: The Economics and Politics of Crisis and Resistance*

Sasha Lilley, *Capital and Its Discontents: Conversations with Radical Thinkers in a Time of Tumult*

Sasha Lilley, David McNally, Eddie Yuen, and James Davis, *Catastrophism: The Apocalyptic Politics of Collapse and Rebirth*

Peter Linebaugh, *Stop, Thief! The Commons, Enclosures, and Resistance*

Peter Linebaugh, *The Incomplete, True, Authentic, and Wonderful History of May Day*

Spectre Classics

E.P. Thompson, *William Morris: Romantic to Revolutionary*

Victor Serge, *Men in Prison*

Victor Serge, *Birth of Our Power*

The Incomplete, True, Authentic, and Wonderful History of May Day

Peter Linebaugh

The Incomplete, True, Authentic, and Wonderful History of May Day
Peter Linebaugh
© 2016 Peter Linebaugh
This edition © 2016 PM Press

ISBN: 978-1-62963-107-3

Library of Congress Control Number: 2015930909

Cover by John Yates / www.stealworks.com
Interior design by briandesign

10 9 8 7 6 5 4 3 2

PM Press
PO Box 23912
Oakland, CA 94623
www.pmpress.org

Printed in the USA

To Robin D.G. Kelley

Contents

ONE

The May Day Punch That Wasn't
Introduction and Acknowledgements
(2015)

Freight Train sprang up from the crowded picnic bench. Sputtering and dumbstruck he stared the professor in the eye, then leaned across the table ready to throw a punch. Our May Day discussion came to an abrupt conclusion.

Freight Train was over six feet in height and 220 pounds in weight. Professor Elwitt, his senior by two or three decades, was a diminutive and unathletic man. As a possible fistfight it was a mismatch.

"They didn't die for me," the professor had said, his lips curling in malice. It was a well-targeted provocation.

Freight Train had just concluded his discourse to the comrades by saying, "they died for us." He was being courteous, restrained in his choice of words, but nevertheless direct and to the point. He recited the names of the martyrs, the leaders of the struggle for the eight-hour day. He told of those who fell to the hysterical violence that the government let loose upon the anarchists of Chicago. He spoke of the call for a general strike on May Day 1886, of the meeting on Haymarket Square a few days later when a stick of dynamite was thrown and a cop killed, of the trial of eight anarchists, of the hanging on "Black Friday," November 11, 1887, when four were hanged—Albert Parsons, George Engel, Adolf Fischer, and August Spies. These were the Haymarket martyrs, *los mártires*, who died for us, as Freight Train said.

We affectionately nicknamed Robert Harmon, the Chicago grad student, "Freight Train," because once he got going you couldn't stop him. He loved the IWW and liked to cast himself in a role familiar to young radicals, "the last of the Wobblies." He had deep loyalties to the Italian American community of Cicero, Illinois, and he'd explain how a combination of the Catholic Church and gangsterism during the 1920s extinguished the hot flame of Italian anarchism. Freight Train's personal mission was to keep that flame alight.

He loved Renaissance history and affected a nonchalance called *sprezzatura*, described in Castiglione's *Book of the Courtier* (1528). Elwitt had been on his PhD oral examination. Freight Train wanted to explain the birthing stool. So he nonchalantly slid off his chair, spread his arms and legs out wide, starfish style, and from a position nearly on the floor, the heels of his shoes grasping the edge of the examining table and supporting his weight, he illustrated to the astonished examiners the posture of parturition as he imagined it to have been during the Italian Renaissance. "This was the way," he explained, "that Machiavelli, Michelangelo, Leonardo da Vinci, and the rest came into the world."

At the examining table and the picnic table alike Freight Train could make history come alive.

In the dimming of the day and the onset of evening, Professor Elwitt, the Marxist, made his way over to the table where we were listening to Freight Train. The professor was a socialist, the student was an anarchist, and they each claimed May Day. Elwitt offered fighting words. At a temporary loss for words himself, the anarchist could only act, and he lunged. It was the Red versus the Black.

A storm in a teacup? Or a near-ritual moment, like a wedding or a funeral, worthy of García Lorca? It was something of both. There was much to it of the academic spat, worthy of a novel of manners, except that to the participants much more was at stake, the weight of history. Or you could see it in another way: it being springtime there were sexual and generational as well as political energies coursing wildly about, not to mention Dionysus with his overflowing cups. The green budding force of winter's end combined with political antagonism of at least a century or two, and the tension was ready to burst. Testosterone bubbled madly in that witch's brew.

Maybe it was the Red and the Green?

We celebrated May Day under a picnic shelter we had rented for the day in the ample and peaceful Ellison Park, Rochester, NY. It was a strictly bring-your-own, potluck affair. We played Capture the Flag across the meadow. Someone with a guitar led us in singing those old labor ballads and civil rights hymns. Beer and wine flowed easily. It was generally laid back, chill. Everyone was usually happy enough. Among the students and workers was the dyer and designer Bethia Waterman, the artist and athlete Joe Hendrick, the brakeman "Disco," and arriving on the back of a motorcycle driven by a lesbian physician, the fierce public health advocate, Michaela Brennan, with whom I was to fall in love. We professors had to put aside our theories and abstractions to speak in a way that even children could understand, so another year we organized a skit for them (as theatre it could hardly be called a play). That was the seed that grew into *The Incomplete, True, Authentic, and Wonderful History of May Day*, as a flyer, a song, and a pamphlet found useful from Boston to San Francisco.

One year we had speeches. Christian Marazzi, a Swiss, all dressed in black leather pants and a black shirt to go with, stood and spoke. His accent and costume were memorable and maybe something too about his analysis of the mysteries of finance capitalism left an impression even if it was incomprehensible to many of us.

In the mid- and late 1970s, having suffered defeats of various kinds, young organizers, activists, radicals, reformers, and revolutionaries heeded the call to study. Back in those days people from all over gravitated to the Rochester History Department to study with its soi-disant Marxists and leftists. If the university was not exactly at the commanding height of the ideological superstructure as the professors imagined it to be, it was certainly one of the sites in the battle of ideas.

In the wake of the great municipal rebellions of the 1960s, led by African Americans, the racist nature of the American university—its curriculum, research, and personnel alike—was clear to all. Some of the professors at the University of Rochester tried to do something about it. Christopher Lasch, Herbert Gutman, Betsy Fox-Genovese, Eugene Genovese, Stanley Engerman were there to teach theory and practice, ideas and action, as we expected. At last these people, these *white* scholars, made academic contributions to Afro-American history. Important book reviews were published, and academic conferences were held for the books. But Marxism, not revolution, was their thing. They were not connected with the workers in the automobile plants, or the welfare mothers of public housing estates, or specific organizations like the League of Revolutionary Black Workers or the Wages for Housework campaign.

A key moment was when Herbert Aptheker, a distinguished member of the Communist Party of the USA, came to campus. He spoke in the Welles-Brown Room. Nobody was willing to introduce him, so they asked the most junior faculty member of the history department without even a PhD to do it, and that was me. Aptheker was running for the U.S. Senate in New York State. He understood what was

4

going on within a pusillanimous history department, and he made the best of a bad situation. He took me aside and told me exactly what to say in my introduction. I was to begin by calling him "doctor," Dr. Herbert Aptheker, and then proceed by naming his major books. I was unfamiliar at the time with his scholarly work, including the classic *American Negro Slave Revolts* (1943). To rectify my own ignorance I began to teach in the maximum-security prison, Attica, at the invitation of its African American Study Group.

Sanford Elwitt was the professor specializing in French labor history, and (what was more relevant) he was the chairman's right-hand man (some said hatchet man) in the department. The chairman was Gene Genovese. These folks had a pretty grandiose idea of themselves. As "revisionists" they were proud not to be stuck with economic determinism. Instead, Genovese had sought to struggle for "hegemony," the buzzword of the Marxist underground of the 1960s, becoming by the 1970s a cross-disciplinary shibboleth of university departments.[1] These Marxists, "Gucci Marxists" we called them for their expensive shoes, were not prepared to treat American slavery as part of the working class.

Yet the truth will out, and it did at that picnic in 1979. A fight in the department had been brewing for a while. Across the table there may have been a partial lunge but certainly the student did not swing. I know because I was in between them at the foot of the table while Freight Train and the professor were on opposite sides. To be sure, tempers flared and faces crimsoned, but flesh did not touch flesh, blood was not spilt. Consequently assault charges were never made, but

---

1   Antonio Gramsci was essential to that moment of the 1960s. John Cammett wrote a biography, John Merrington introduced him in *Socialist Register*, and Trevor Griffiths wrote theatre about him then playing in London.

later the history department met and voted to expel Freight Train. It was the beginning of the end for me too.

But not before another May Day when I sang an old English Labour Party song I had been taught as a child in England: to the tune of "The Battle Hymn of the Republic,"

> We will make the Dean of Canterbury Speaker of the House (3 *times*)
> When the Red Revolution comes!

"The Red Dean" of Canterbury was Hewlett Johnson (1874–1966), a Church of England priest and a Stalinist through and through. The problem came with the chorus, which was belted out with a full ironic, beery shout:

> Arson, rape, and bloody murder

it went, and then the line was repeated, only louder and even more obnoxiously. "Political correctness" had not yet been formulated as a devastating phrase but the thing itself was alive and healthy. This led later to an informal gathering among feminists to raise my consciousness and explain that such a sentiment could not be uttered even in jest given the realities of violence against women. Humbled if not humiliated, I learned my lesson and have not sung it since. It is a foolish line even as a beer-driven music-hall shout.

What is to be our relationship to the Red or the Communist and Socialist traditions? Some things we want to keep from the past, and others to discard. Our class has a tradition of arson—think of the fire of the sugar plantations, think of the arson in the English agrarian, "moral economy," riots, and during some periods of history assassination or execution has been employed against class enemies—Robert Frost even has a poem about it, but rape, as I have learned from Andrea Smith, has always been a tool, an initial and necessary tool she would argue, of imperialism. Political principle can be strengthened by knowledge of the sacrifices in the past. This didn't mean we had to think *exactly* as they did, or sing with the same rough humor.

Later I moved to Boston. I wanted to preserve a tradition, to carry forward the lessons I had learned from the feminists of Rochester, from the African Americans of Attica, as well as the labor history of the Marxists, and the anarchist history of Freight Train. At Tufts University I met wonderful comrades in the antiapartheid struggle such as John Roosa, Bryn Clark, and Dan Coughlin. Dave Riker as part of Somerville Community Television had me talk about May Day. In Boston I wrote "The Silent Speak." In 1986 we organized the first ever University of Massachusetts celebration of May Day. I want to describe the persons and places because they became part of the global awakening to May Day. These are the people of the movement that I thank directly as inspiration for the essays below.

I invited George Rawick to speak at Law Day, as May Day was officially called. I invited him because a) he edited about two dozen volumes of the American slave narratives, and b) he was closely associated with the anticapitalist projects of C.L.R. James and the former Facing Reality group. He was fantastic because he reminded us how people can change. His example was Albert Parsons, who had been a Confederate cavalry officer defending the slave South, and then became husband to Lucy Parsons and an abolitionist of chattel slavery and wage slavery alike. Politically, Parsons was a socialist, an anarchist, and a trade unionist all rolled into one. So who's normal, Rawick wanted to know.

We had some local Morris dancers, the Black Jokers, with bells on their ankles and ribbons from their hats, do that English folk dance dating back to 1458. Named after Moors! They danced "to wake up the earth." A Somerville blues band, the Wicked Casuals, provided music. Soon everyone was shouting. We rented a small motor launch and sailed over to Quincy where the first Maypole in North America was erected in 1626.

On board our little ship a Brazilian band, El Echo, supplied gentle music. Dieri from Haiti came along. Teodros Kiros of Ethiopia joined us. Our indigenous comrade, Johnny Mañana of Peru, and his partner, Nancy Kelly, joined us. Sal Salerno had copies of *The Haymarket Scrapbook* for distribution. Randall Conrad embarked along with Christine and their child, Pete. Randall made a terrific film called *3,000 Years and Life* about the time when the prisoners ruled the maximum-security prison in Walpole, Massachusetts. He made another one too, *A Little Rebellion Now and Then*, about Shays' Rebellion of 1786–87.

Margot Fitzgerald spoke on behalf of the work-study students whose pay "had run out." She called for a one-day work stoppage. Charlie Shively, the historian and gay rights advocate, read a poem about death row, and in words from Walt Whitman expressed our duty to "Cheer up slaves, Horrify despots!" Monty Neill gave a terrific speech explaining the rainbow coalition of Merry Mount. Noel Ignatiev, who used to work at International Harvester in Chicago, gave us the inside story of the Haymarket bombing.

That year there was a boycott of Shell Oil, a parade to the shantytown against apartheid up on Harvard Yard, and a sit-in in Cambridge as well. By late afternoon news came to us, even at sea, that millions of people in South Africa were on strike. We sent greetings to them and to the people near Chernobyl in Ukraine. The art students at Massachusetts College marched to Boston Common chanting praises for the Nicaraguan revolution while Duncan Kenney lectured the Harvard Economics Department on "the fetishism of commodities."

May Day is about affirmation, the love of life, and the start of spring, so it has to be about the beginning of the end of the capitalist system of exploitation, oppression, misery, toil, and moil. Besides full affirmation May Day requires denunciation: the denunciation of capitalism, of patriarchy, of homophobia, of white supremacy, of war. For me Rochester had been about receiving this knowledge, and Boston about transmitting it.

The essays in this book are all occasional essays (of course), and most were written the night or week before the occasion. They were written during decades of conservative repression when celebrations of Haymarket were few and far between. The title essay was published under the imprimatur of Midnight Notes, an anticapitalist collective that was also struggling to express itself during those leaden times. "May Day Meditation" referred to the *Auroras of the Zapatistas*, a book by Midnight Notes. I printed "X^2" in a miniscule format and passed it out willy-nilly on street corners and at sporting events. Six of these essays were published in the online magazine *CounterPunch*, so I thank especially Jeffrey St. Clair. Special thanks also to Jeff Clark, who published "Ypsilanti Vampire May Day." "Obama May Day" was republished in the second edition of Dave Roediger and Franklin Rosemont's indispensable *Haymarket Scrapbook*.

The essay following this one ("The Incomplete, True, Authentic, and Wonderful History of May Day") was first published as a pamphlet, some copies having a green and others having a red cover to indicate its two themes, nature and labor. The Green is presented as Robin Goodfellow, the subversive spirit of the land at the time of the giant enclosures when state-sponsored monotheism sought to root out pantheism and capitalism destroyed the commons. The last essay, "Swan Honk," also has the Red theme of labor. Otherwise the Green theme is replaced by a geological rather than an agrarian perspective. It thus includes eons of time prior to the agrarian or the Neolithic with its empires and

9

the religions of the "axial age." It is dated April 30, not May Day, because bureaucrats wouldn't let me date my retirement on May Day; it had to be the day before.

You'll find no picnic in "Swan Honk" nor will you find a punch. May Day is no longer as dogmatic as "the punch that wasn't" seemed to imply, neither a USA-USSR ding-dong, nor a brawl of fisticuffs between anarchists and Marxists. May Day, dear comrade-reader, like the author of these pieces, is nowadays both bolder and more open to new meanings than before. To balance the machismo of that unthrown punch at the start of this intro, we might end with a deep note of anti-imperialist sisterhood from two expectant mothers from the axial age, Elizabeth and Mary. Mary's "magnificat" anticipated an *individual messiah* where we might struggle instead for a *revolutionary class* whose solemn vow and every action is to rout the arrogant of heart and mind, to bring down the mighty from their thrones, to lift up the humble, to satisfy the hungry with good things, and to send the rich empty away. That, the commons, and the eight-hour day!

TWO

The Incomplete, True, Authentic, and Wonderful History of May Day

(1986)

The Soviet government parades missiles and marches soldiers on May Day. The American government has called May 1 "Loyalty Day" and associates it with militarism. The real meaning of this day has been obscured by the designing propaganda of both governments. The truth of May Day is totally different. To the history of May Day there is a Green side and there is a Red side.

Under the rainbow, our methodology must be colorful. Green is a relationship to the earth and what grows therefrom. Red is a relationship to other people and the blood spilt there among. Green designates life with only necessary labor; Red designates death with surplus labor. Green is natural appropriation; Red is social expropriation. Green is husbandry and nurturance; Red is proletarianization and prostitution. Green is useful activity; Red is useless toil. Green is creation of desire; Red is class struggle. May Day is both.

The Green

Once upon a time, long before Weinberger bombed North Africans, before the Bank of Boston laundered money, or Reagan honored the Nazi war dead, the earth was blanketed by a broad mantle of forests. As late as Caesar's time a person might travel through the woods for two months without gaining an unobstructed view of the sky. The immense forests of Europe, Asia, Africa, and America provided the atmosphere with oxygen and the earth with nutrients. Within the woodland ecology our ancestors did not have to work the graveyard shift, or deal with flextime, or work from Nine to Five. Indeed, the Native Americans whom Captain John Smith encountered in 1606 only worked four hours a week. The origin of May Day is to be found in the Woodland Epoch of History.

In Europe, as in Africa, people honored the woods in many ways. With the leafing of the trees in spring, people celebrated "the fructifying spirit of vegetation," to use the phrase of J.G. Frazer, the anthropologist. They did this in May, a month named after Maia, the mother of all the gods according to the ancient Greeks, giving birth even to Zeus.

The Greeks had their sacred groves, the Druids their oak worship, the Romans their games in honor of Floralia. In Scotland the herdsmen formed circles and danced around fires. The Celts lit bonfires in hilltops to honor their god, Beltane. In the Tyrol people let their dogs bark and made music with pots and pans. In Scandinavia fires were lit and the witches came out.

Everywhere people "went a-Maying" by going into the woods and bringing back leaf, bough, and blossom to decorate their persons, homes, and loved ones with green garlands. Outside theatre was performed with characters like "Jack-in-the-Green" and the "Queen of the May." Trees were planted. Maypoles were erected. Dances were danced. Music was played. Drinks were drunk, and love was made. Winter was over, spring had sprung.

The history of these customs is complex and affords the student of the past with many interesting insights into the history of religion, gender, reproduction, and village ecology.

Take Joan of Arc who was burned in May 1431. Her inquisitors believed she was a witch. Not far from her birthplace, she told the judges, "There is a tree that they call 'The Ladies' Tree'—others call it 'The Fairies' Tree.' It is a beautiful tree, from which comes the Maypole. I have sometimes been to play with the young girls to make garlands for Our Lady of Domrémy. Often I have heard the old folk say that the fairies haunt this tree." In the general indictment against Joan, one of the particulars against her was dressing like a man. The paganism of Joan's heresy originated in the Old Stone Age when religion was animistic and shamans were women and men.

Monotheism arose with the Mediterranean empires. Even the most powerful Roman Empire had to make deals with its conquered and enslaved peoples (syncretism). As it destroyed some customs, it had to accept or transform others. Thus, we have Christmas trees. May Day became a day to honor the saints, Philip and James, who were unwilling slaves to Empire. James the Less neither drank nor shaved. He spent so much time praying that he developed huge calluses on his knees, likening them to camel legs. Philip was a lazy guy. When Jesus said "Follow me" Philip tried to get out of it by saying he had to tend to his father's funeral, and it was to this excuse that the carpenter's son made his famous reply, "Let the dead bury the dead." James was stoned to death, and Philip was crucified head downward. Their martyrdom introduces the Red side of the story, even still the Green side is preserved because, according to the floral directory, the tulip is dedicated to Philip and bachelor buttons to James.

The farmers, workers, and child bearers (laborers) of the Middle Ages had hundreds of holy days which preserved the May Green, despite the attack on peasants and witches. Despite the complexities, whether May Day was observed by sacred or profane ritual, by pagan or Christian, by magic or not, by straights or gays, by gentle or calloused hands, it was always a celebration of all that is free and life-giving in the world. That is the Green side of the story. Whatever else it was, it was not a time to work.

Therefore, it was attacked by the authorities. The repression had begun with the burning of women and it continued in the sixteenth century when America was "discovered," the slave trade was begun, and nation-states and capitalism were formed. In 1550 an Act of Parliament demanded that Maypoles be destroyed, and it outlawed games. In 1644 the Puritans in England abolished May Day altogether. To these work-ethicists the festival was obnoxious for paganism and worldliness. Philip Stubbs, for example, in *The Anatomy of Abuses* (1583) wrote of the Maypole, "and then fall they to banquet and feast, to leape and daunce about it, as the Heathen people did at the dedication of their Idolles." When a Puritan mentioned "heathen" we know genocide was not far away. According to the excellent slide show at the Quincy Historical Society, 90 percent of the Massachusetts people, including Chief Chicatabat, died from chicken pox or small pox a few years after the Puritans landed in 1619. The Puritans also objected to the unrepressed sexuality of the day. Stubbs said, "Of fourtie, threescore, or an hundred maides going to the wood, there have scarcely the third part of them returned home again as they went."

The people resisted the repressions. Thenceforth, they called their May sports the "Robin Hood Games." Capering about with sprigs of hawthorn in their hair and bells jangling from their knees, the ancient characters of May were transformed into an outlaw community, Maid Marians and Little Johns. The May feast was presided over by the "Lord of Misrule," "the King of Unreason," or the "Abbot of Inobedience." Washington Irving was later to write that the feeling for May "has become chilled by habits of gain and traffic." As the gainers and traffickers sought to impose the regimen of monotonous work, the people responded to preserve their holyday. Thus began in earnest the Red side of the story of May Day. The struggle was brought to Massachusetts in 1626.

Thomas Morton of Merry Mount

In 1625 Captain Wollaston, Thomas Morton, and thirty others sailed from England and months later, taking their bearings from a red cedar tree, they disembarked in Quincy Bay. A year later Wollaston, impatient for lucre and gain, left for good to Virginia. Thomas Morton settled in Passonaggessit, which he named Merry Mount. The land seemed a "Paradise" to him. He wrote, there are "fowls in abundance, fish in multitudes, and I discovered besides, millions of turtle doves on the green boughs, which sat pecking of the full, ripe, pleasant grapes that were supported by the lusty trees, whose fruitful load did cause the arms to bend."

On May Day, 1627, he and his Indian friends, stirred by the sound of drums, erected a Maypole eighty feet high, decorated it with garlands, wrapped it in ribbons, and nailed to its top the antlers of a buck. Later he wrote that he "sett up a Maypole upon the festival day of Philip and James, and therefore brewed a barrell of excellent beare." A ganymede sang a Bacchanalian song. Morton attached to the pole the first lyric verses penned in America which concluded:

> With the proclamation that the first of May
> At Merry Mount shall be kept holly day

The Puritans at Plymouth were opposed to May Day. They called the Maypole "an Idoll" and named Merry Mount "Mount Dagon" after the god of the first oceangoing imperialists, the Phoenicians. More likely, though, the Puritans were the imperialists, not Morton, who worked with slaves, servants, and Native Americans, person to person. Everyone was equal in his "social contract." Governor Bradford wrote, "they allso set up a Maypole, drinking and dancing aboute it many days together, inviting the Indean women for thier consorts, dancing and frisking together (like so many faires, or furies rather) and worse practise."

Merry Mount became a refuge for Indians, the discontented, gay people, runaway servants, and what the governor called "all the scume of the countrie." When the authorities reminded him that his actions violated the King's Proclamation, Morton replied that it was "no law." Miles Standish, whom Morton called "Mr. Shrimp," attacked. The Maypole was cut down. The settlement was burned. Morton's goods were confiscated; he was chained in the bilboes, and ostracized to England aboard the ship *The Gift* at a cost, the Puritans complained, of twelve pounds seven shillings. The rainbow coalition of Merry Mount was thus destroyed for the time being. That Merry Mount later (1636) became associated with Anne Hutchinson, the famous midwife, spiritualist, and feminist, surely was more than coincidental. Her brother-in-law ran the Chapel of Ease. She thought that God loved everybody, regardless of their sins. She doubted the Puritans' authority to make law. A statue of Robert Burns in Quincy near to Merry Mount quotes the poet's lines,

> A fig for those by law protected!
> Liberty's a glorious feast!
> Courts for cowards were erected,
> Churches built to please the priest.

Thomas Morton was a thorn in the side of the Boston and Plymouth Puritans, because he had an alternate vision of Massachusetts. He was impressed by its fertility; they by its scarcity. He befriended the Indians; they shuddered at the thought. He was egalitarian; they proclaimed themselves the "Elect." He freed servants; they lived off them. He armed the Indians; they used arms against Indians. To Nathaniel Hawthorne, the destiny of American settlement was decided at Merry Mount. Casting the struggle as mirth vs. gloom, grizzly saints vs. gay sinners, green vs. iron, it was the Puritans who won, and the fate of America was determined in favor of psalm-singing, Indian-scalpers whose notion of the Maypole was a whipping post.

Parts of the past live, parts die. The red cedar that drew Morton first to Merry Mount blew down in the gale of 1898. A section of it, about eight feet of its trunk, became a power fetish in 1919, placed as it was next to the president's chair of the Quincy City Council. Interested parties may now view it in the Quincy History Museum. Living trees, however, have since grown, despite the closure of the shipyards.

On Both Sides of the Atlantic

In England the attacks on May Day were a necessary part of the wearisome, unending attempt to establish industrial work discipline. The attempt was led by the Puritans with their belief that toil was godly and less toil wicked. Absolute surplus value could be increased only by increasing the hours of labor and abolishing holydays. A parson wrote a piece of work propaganda called "Funebria Florae, Or the Downfall of the May Games." He attacked "ignorants, atheists, papists, drunkards, swearers, swashbucklers, maidmarians, morrice-dancers, maskers, mummers, Maypole stealers, health-drinkers, together with a rapscallion rout of fiddlers, fools, fighters, gamesters, lewd men, light women, contemners of magistracy, affronters of ministry, rebellious to masters, disobedients to parents, misspenders of time, and abusers of the creature, &c."

At about this time, Isaac Newton, the gravitationist and machinist of time, said work was a law of planets and apples alike. Thus work ceased to be merely the ideology of the Puritans; it became a law of the universe. In 1717 Newton purchased London's hundred-foot Maypole and used it to prop up his telescope.

Chimney sweeps and dairymaids led the resistance. The sweeps dressed up as women on May Day, or put on aristocratic periwigs. They sang songs and collected money. When the Earl of Bute in 1763 refused to pay, the opprobrium was so great that he was forced to resign. Milk maids used to go a-Maying by dressing in floral garlands, dancing, and getting the dairymen to distribute their milk-yield freely. Soot and milk workers thus helped to retain the holyday right into the industrial revolution.

The ruling class used the day for its own purposes. Thus, when Parliament was forced to abolish slavery in the British dominions, it did so on May Day 1807. In 1820 the Cato Street conspirators plotted to destroy the British cabinet while it was having dinner. Irish, Jamaican, and Cockney were hanged for the attempt on May Day 1820. A conspirator wrote his wife saying, "Justice and liberty have taken their flight . . . to other distant shores." He meant America, where Boston Brahmin, Robber Baron, and Southern Plantocrat divided and ruled an arching rainbow of people.

Two bands of that rainbow came from English and Irish islands. One was Green. Robert Owen, union leader, socialist, and founder of utopian communities in America, announced the beginning of the millennium after May Day 1833. The other was Red. On May Day 1830, a founder of the Knights of Labor, the United Mine Workers of America, and the Wobblies was born in Ireland, Mary Harris Jones, a.k.a. "Mother Jones." She was a Maia of the American working class.

May Day continued to be commemorated in America, one way or another, despite the victory of the Puritans at

Merry Mount. On May Day 1779 the revolutionaries of Boston confiscated the estates of "enemies of Liberty." On May Day 1808 "twenty different dancing groups of the wretched Africans" in New Orleans danced to the tunes of their own drums until sunset when the slave patrols showed themselves with their cutlasses. "The principal dancers or leaders are dressed in a variety of wild and savage fashions, always ornamented with a number of tails of the small wild beasts," observed a strolling white man.

The Red: Haymarket

The history of the modern May Day originates in the center of the North American plains, at Haymarket, in Chicago—"the city on the make"—in May 1886. The Red side of that story is more well-known than the Green, because it was bloody. But there was also a Green side to the tale, though the green was not so much that of pretty grass garlands, as it was of greenbacks, for in Chicago, it was said, the dollar is king.

Of course the prairies are green in May. Virgin soil, dark, brown, crumbling, shot with fine black sand, it was the produce of thousands of years of humus and organic decomposition. For many centuries this earth was husbanded by the Native Americans of the plains. As Black Elk said, theirs is "the story of all life that is holy and is good to tell, and of us two-leggeds sharing in it with the four-leggeds and the wings of the air and all green things; for these are children of one mother and their father is one Spirit." From such a green perspective, the white men appeared as pharaohs, and indeed, as Abe Lincoln put it, these prairies were the "Egypt of the West."

The land was mechanized. Relative surplus value could only be obtained by reducing the price of food. The proteins and vitamins of this fertile earth spread through the whole world. Chicago was the jugular vein. Cyrus McCormick wielded the surgeon's knife. His mechanical reapers harvested the grasses and grains. McCormick produced 1,500 reapers in 1849; by 1884 he was producing 80,000. Not that McCormick actually made reapers; members of the Molders Union Local 23 did that, and on May Day 1867 they went on strike, starting the eight-hour movement.

A staggering transformation was wrought. It was: "Farewell" to the hammer and sickle. "Goodbye" to the cradle scythe. "So long" to Emerson's man with the hoe. These now became the artifacts of nostalgia and romance. It became "Hello" to the hobo. "Move on" to the harvest stiffs. "Line up" the proletarians. Such were the new commands of civilization.

Thousands of immigrants, many from Germany, poured into Chicago after the Civil War. Class war was advanced, technically and logistically. In 1855 the Chicago police used Gatling guns against the workers who protested the closing of the beer gardens. In the Bread Riot of 1872, the police clubbed hungry people in a tunnel under the river. In the 1877 railway strike, federal troops fought workers at the Battle of the Viaduct. These troops were recently seasoned from fighting the Sioux who had killed Custer. Henceforth, the defeated Sioux could only "Go to a mountain top and cry for a vision." The Pinkerton Detective Agency put visions into practice by teaching the city police how to spy and to form fighting columns for deployment in city streets. A hundred years ago during the streetcar strike, the police issued a shoot-to-kill order.

McCormick cut wages 15 percent. His profit rate was 71 percent. In May 1886 four molders whom McCormick locked out were shot dead by the police. Thus did this "grim reaper" maintain his profits.

Nationally, May First 1886 was important because a couple of years earlier the Federation of Organized

Trade and Labor Unions of the United States and Canada, "RESOLVED … that eight hours shall constitute a legal day's labor, from and after May 1, 1886."

On May 4, 1886, several thousand people gathered near Haymarket Square to hear what August Spies, a newspaperman, had to say about the shootings at the McCormick Works. Albert Parsons, a typographer and labor leader, spoke next. Later, at his trial, he said, "What is Socialism or Anarchism? Briefly stated it is the right of the toilers to the free and equal use of the tools of production and the right of the producers to their product." He was followed by "Good-Natured Sam" Fielden who as a child had worked in the textile factories of Lancashire, England. He was a Methodist preacher and labor organizer. He got done speaking at 10:30 p.m. At that time 176 policemen charged the crowd that had dwindled to about 200. An unknown hand threw a stick of dynamite, the first time that Alfred Nobel's invention was used in class battle.

All hell broke loose, many were killed, and the rest is history.

"Make the raids first and look up the law afterwards," was the sheriff's dictum. It was followed religiously across the country. Newspapers screamed for blood, homes were ransacked, and suspects were subjected to the "third degree." Eight men were railroaded in Chicago at a farcical trial. Four men hanged on "Black Friday," November 11, 1887.

"There will come a time when our silence will be more powerful than the voices you strangle today," said Spies before he choked.

May Day Since 1886

Lucy Parsons, widowed by Chicago's "just-us," was born in Texas. She was partly Afro-American, partly Native American, and partly Hispanic. She set out to tell the world the true story "of one whose only crime was that he lived in advance of his time." She went to England and encouraged English workers to make May Day an international holiday for shortening the hours of work. Her friend William Morris wrote a poem called "May Day."

> *Workers:* They are few, we are many: and yet, O our Mother,
> Many years were wordless and nought was our deed,
> But now the word flitteth from brother to brother:
> We have furrowed the acres and scattered the seed.
>
> *Earth:* Win on then unyielding, through fair and foul weather,
> And pass not a day that your deed shall avail.
> And in hope every spring-tide come gather together
> That unto the Earth ye may tell all your tale.

Her work was not in vain. May Day, or "The Day of the Chicago Martyrs" as it is still called in Mexico, "belongs to the working class and is dedicated to the revolution," as Eugene Debs put it in his May Day editorial of 1907. The A.F. of L. declared it a holiday. Sam Gompers sent an emissary to Europe to have it proclaimed an international labor day. Both the Knights of Labor and the Second International officially adopted the day. Bismarck, on the other hand, outlawed May Day. President Grover Cleveland announced that the first Monday in September would be Labor Day in America, as he tried to divide the international working class. Huge numbers were out of work, and they began marching. Under the generalship of Jacob Coxey they descended on Washington, DC, on May Day 1894, the first big march on Washington. Two years later across the world Lenin wrote an important May Day pamphlet for the Russian factory workers in 1896. The Russian Revolution of 1905 began on May Day.

With the success of the 1917 Bolshevik Revolution the Red side of May Day became scarlet, crimson, for ten million people were slaughtered in World War I. The end of the war brought work stoppages, general strikes, and insurrections all over the world, from Mexico to Kenya, from China to France. In Boston on May Day 1919 the young telephone workers threatened to strike, and twenty thousand workers in Lawrence went on strike again for the eight-hour day. There were fierce clashes between working people and police in Cleveland as well as in other cities on May Day of that year. A lot of socialists, anarchists, Bolsheviks, Wobblies, and other "I-Won't-Workers" ended up in jail as a result.

This didn't get them down. At "Wire City," as they called the federal pen at Fort Leavenworth, there was a grand parade and no work on May Day 1919. Pictures of Lenin and Lincoln were tied to the end of broomsticks and held afloat. There were speeches and songs. *The Liberator* supplies us with an account of the day, but it does not tell us who won the Wobbly-Socialist horseshoe-throwing contest. Nor does it tell us what happened to the soldier caught waving a red ribbon from the guards' barracks. Meanwhile, one mile underground in the copper mines of Bisbee where there are no national boundaries, Spanish-speaking Americans were singing "The Internationale" on May Day.

In the 1920s and 1930s the day was celebrated by union organizers, the unemployed, and determined workers. In New York City the big May Day celebration was held in Union Square. In the 1930s Lucy Parsons marched in Chicago on May Day with her young friend, Studs Terkel. On May Day 1946 the Arabs began a general strike in Palestine, and the Jews of the Displaced Persons Camps in Landsberg, Germany, went on hunger strike. On May Day 1947 autoworkers in Paris downed tools, an insurrection in Paraguay broke out, the Mafia killed six May Day marchers in Sicily, and the Boston Parks' commissioner said that this was the first year in living memory when neither Communist nor Socialist had applied for a permit to rally on the Common.

Nineteen sixty-eight was a good year for May Day. Allen Ginsberg was made the "Lord of Misrule" in Prague before the Russians got there. In London hundreds of students lobbied Parliament against a bill to stop Third World immigration into England. In Mississippi police could not prevent 350 black students from supporting their jailed friends. At Columbia University thousands of students petitioned against armed police on campus. In Detroit with the help of the Dodge Revolutionary Union Movement, the first wildcat strike in fifteen years took place at the Hamtramck Assembly Plant (Dodge Main), against speedup. In Cambridge, Massachusetts, black leaders advocated police reforms while in New York the mayor signed a bill providing the police with the most sweeping "emergency" powers known in American history. The climax to the '68 Mai was reached in France where there was a gigantic general strike under strange slogans such as

Parlez a vos voisins!
L'Imagination prend le pouvoir!
Dessous les pavés c'est la plage!

On May Day in 1971 President Nixon couldn't sleep. He ordered ten thousand paratroopers and marines to Washington, DC, because he was afraid that some people calling themselves the May Day Tribe might succeed in their goal of blocking access to the Department of Justice. In the Philippines four students were shot to death protesting the dictatorship. In Boston Mayor White argued against the right of municipal workers, including the police, to withdraw their services or stop working. In May 1980 we may see Green themes in Mozambique where the workers lamented the absence of beer, or in Germany where three hundred women witches rampaged through Hamburg. Red themes may be seen in the thirty thousand Brazilian autoworkers who struck, or in the 5.8 million Japanese who struck against inflation.

On May Day 1980 the Green and Red themes were combined when a former Buick automaker from Detroit, one "Mr. Toad," sat at a picnic table and penned the following lines,

The eight-hour day is not enough;
We are thinking of more and better stuff.
So here is our prayer and here is our plan,
We want what we want and we'll take what we can.

Down with wars both small and large,
Except for the ones where we're in charge:
Those are the wars of class against class,
Where we get a chance to kick some ass.

For air to breathe and water to drink,
And no more poison from the kitchen sink.
For land that's green and life that's saved
And less and less of the earth that's paved.

No more women who are less than free,
Or men who cannot learn to see
Their power steals their humanity
And makes us all less than we can be.

For teachers who learn and students who teach
And schools that are kept beyond the reach
Of provosts and deans and chancellors and such
And Xerox and Kodak and Shell, Royal Dutch.

An end to shops that are dark and dingy,
An end to Bosses whether good or stingy,
An end to work that produces junk,
An end to junk that produces work,
And an end to all in charge—the jerks.

For all who dance and sing, loud cheers,
To the prophets of doom we send some jeers,
To our friends and lovers we give free beers,
And to all who are here, a day without fears.

So, on this first of May we all should say
That we will either make it or break it.
Or, to put this thought another way,
Let's take it easy, but let's take it.

Law Day USA

Yet May Day was always a troubling day in America; some wished to forget it. In 1939 Pennsylvania declared it "Americanism Day." In 1947 Congress declared it to be "Loyalty Day." Yet these attempts to hide the meaning of the day have never succeeded. As the Wobblies say, "We Never Forget."

Likewise in 1958, at the urging of Charles Rhyne, May 1 was proclaimed "Law Day USA." As a result the politicians had another opportunity for bombast about the Cold War and to tout their own virtues. Senator Javits, for instance, took a deep historical breath in May 1960 by saying American ideas were the highest "ever espoused since the dawn of civilization." Governor Rockefeller of New York got right to his point by saying that the traditional May Day "bordered on treason." As an activity for the day Senator Wiley recommended that people read statute books. In preaching on "Obedience to Authority" on May Day 1960, the chaplain of the Senate believed it was the first time in the twentieth century that the subject had been addressed. He reminded people of the words carved on the courthouse in Worcester, Massachusetts: "Obedience to Law is Liberty." He said God is "all law" and suggested we sing the hymn, "Make Me a Captive, Lord [and then I shall be free]." He complained that

TV shows made fun of cops and husbands. He said God had become too maternal.

Beneath the hypocrisy of such talk (at the time the Senate was rejecting the jurisdiction of the World Court), there were indications of the revolt in the kitchens. In addition to the trumpeting Cold War overtones, frightened patriarchal undertones were essential to the Law Day music. Indeed, it attempted to drown out both the Red and the Green. Those who have to face the law-and-order music on a daily basis, the lawyers and the orderers, also have to make their own deals.

Among the lawyers there are conservatives and liberals; they are generally ideologues. On Law Day 1964 the president of the Connecticut Bar wrote against civil rights demonstrators, "corrupt" labor unions, "juvenile delinquency," and Liz Taylor! William O. Douglas, on the other hand, on Law Day 1962 warned against mimicking British imperialism and favored independence movements and the Peace Corps by saying, "We need Michigan-in-Nigeria, California-in-the-Congo, Columbia-in-Iran," which has come true, at least judging by what's written on sweatshirts around the world. Neither the conservative nor the liberal, however, said it should be a holiday for the lawyers, nor did they advocate the eight-hour day for the workers of the legal apparatus. In Boston only the New England School of Law, the Law and Justice Program at UMass., and the College of Public and Community Service celebrate the Green and the Red.

Among the orderers (the police) Law Day isn't much of a holiday either. Yet police, men and women, all over the United States owe a lot to May Day and the Boston police. It is true that more than a thousand Boston men of blue lost their jobs owing to Calvin Coolidge's suppression of the Boston police strike of 1919. They had been busy earlier in the summer during May Day. At the same time there were lasting gains: a small pay increase ($300 a year), shorter hours (73–90 a week had been the norm), and most important, free uniforms!

An Ending

Where is the Red and Green today? Is it in Mao's *Red Book*? Or in Col. Khadafy's *Green Book*? Some perhaps. Leigh Hunt, the English essayist of the nineteenth century, wrote that May Day is "the union of the two best things in the world, the love of nature, and the love of each other." Certainly, such Green union is possible, because we all can imagine it, and we know that what is real now was once only imagined. Just as certainly, that union can be realized only by Red struggle, because there is no gain without pain, as the aerobiticians say, or no dreams without responsibility, no birth without labor, no Green without Red.

The children used to celebrate May Day. I think schools stopped encouraging them sometime around when "Law Day" was created, but I'm not sure. A correspondent from East Arlington, Massachusetts, writes that in the late 1940s, "On any given Saturday in May, anywhere from 10–30 children would dress up in crepe paper costumes (hats, shirts, &c.); we would pick baskets of flowers and parade up and down several streets (until the flowers ran out!) The whole time we would be chanting, 'May Party, May Party, rah, rah, rah!' A leader would be chosen, but I don't remember how. (Probably by throwing fingers out). Then, we would parade up to Spy Pond at the edge of the Center off Lake Street and have a picnic lunch." This correspondent now teaches kindergarten. "In recent years," she continues, "I have always decorated a May Pole for my kindergarten class (they do the decorations actually), and we would dance around it. It would always attract attention from the older children."

THREE

X²: May Day in Light of Waco and LA

(1993)

X stands for the unknown. Hence, Malcolm Little chose it to replace his slave name when he awoke to political consciousness, Malcolm X. It became an ever-present reminder of slavery days and the theft of land and identity. X means other things as well. It marks the spot. It can be a signature. In math it stands for an unknown quantity; in politics it stands for an unknown quality.

To Karl Marx there was a "secret" to accumulation, something unknown, so, we may name it X. It stands for expropriation. Expropriation is the taking away of what's ours, such as the rainforest, or the land. It happens all over the world, in particular in Haiti, in Somalia, in Guatemala, in the Philippines, and the World Bank plans it for Papua New Guinea. This expropriation has also happened in Europe and North America. It is an unknown quality because the ruling class pretends it doesn't happen. Karl Marx spoke of a second X, exploitation. Exploitation coerces us to work without being paid. Since unpaid labor is the be-all and end-all of capitalism, the source of profit, interest, and rent, the capitalist likes to hide it too, and pretends that it doesn't exist either. Despite the fact it kills us, exploitation is an unknown quantity. To comprehend May Day we need to understand both expropriation and exploitation. We need to make them known. May Day has been against both. Hence, X^2.

May Day falls between winter (death) and summer (life). Being spring, it is time to review the past and look where we're headed. In light of last weekend, this is a grim business. On the one hand, there was the massive police and military mobilization in Los Angeles in anticipation of a repetition of the Great Uprising of 1992. On the other hand, there was the holocaust at Waco, Texas, with the lethal consumption of the Branch Davidians by fire whose ignition occurred under circumstances determined by the FBI.

Apparently, they didn't have much to do with each other. The Davidians thought Earth was Hell and they sought a new Jerusalem when "there shall be no more death, neither sorrow nor crying; neither shall there be any more pain, for the former things are passed away." The Angelenos sought Heaven on Earth and they were going to take both justice and wealth into their own hands by direct action and the fire this time. One was all book and too much religion; the other was irreligious with not enough book. One was a cult of the boonies, the other was a culture of the inner city. One was an uprising of the proletariat; the other was a massacre of religious fanatics. The media spent millions proving the lack of virtue in each: the Angelenos were driven by greed, revenge, and drugs, while the Davidians were motivated by frenzy, lust, and rock 'n' roll.

Dialectics and prophecy alike teach us to search beneath the surface. Cornell West says the first quality of prophecy is discernment, or the ability to look into the roots, to analyze the history. Furthermore, history must be from "the vantage point of those below," because truth emerges only with suffering. Dialectics teaches that every question has two sides—the capitalist side and the class side. We must look at the roots from the vantage of those below for a dialectical reason: creativity resides below, inevitability above. The World Bank and the IMF looked at LA and said it was the future: urban explosions may be anticipated for the coming century, as education, energy, water, health, and food are reduced for the big cities (*Los Angeles Times*, May 25, 1992). But the Uprising of 1992 caught everybody by surprise, and it caught on too, in Toronto, Lagos, Panama, and forty-four other cities. Capital drew a lesson of scarcity, inevitability, and determinism; or What Is, Has to Be. Our class drew a lesson of creativity, possibility, and freedom.

Both are stories of capital punishment, death. Both are stories whose protagonists are international and multicultural. The two stories are linked in police science: "Ms. Reno decided to approve the FBI's plan on Saturday evening, after a long meeting in her office with senior aides who had been euphoric and relieved over the verdicts earlier in the day in the Rodney King beating case" (*New York Times*, April 21, 1993). Are the roots deeper? Let us take a walk into history.

A walk, I say, not a stroll with the head in the air like the New Agers, nor a dawdle, with the Romantic Samuel Coleridge, who originated the dreamy approach. One thousand years ago the Anglo-Saxons (his tribe) met to chose the wise men, or *wits*, at Whitsuntide during the "folk motes" when a truce of the Goddess was observed, when the people met around the common green and Maypole, electing a king and a queen, he an oaken and she a hawthorn wreath, and when they enjoyed a Saturnalia for the sake of fertility. So, May Day began long ago, in the Woodland epoch of history, long before there was expropriation. Was that the gay time of dances and games, of love and kisses? Yes, it was. Coleridge then jumped over a thousand years to his own day, 1796, and said that the Maypole was just the same as the English Tree of Liberty.

But with that jump he misses the whole point. He omits all expropriation. He says nothing of the slave trade. He says nothing of conquest. He says nothing of war. The New Age wants rain without thunder; the Romantic wants fertility without lightning. He omits X^2 and says nothing of the enclosures, which expropriated people from the village common. The enclosures began with Henry VIII, the wife murderer, during whose reign, the old chronicles say, seventy-two thousand were hanged. The people had a choice: they could flee to the inner city, London, or they could become boat people and migrate beyond the seas. Either way they became vagabonds.

The enclosures have not stopped. Read *Midnight Oil: Work, Energy, War: 1973–1992*. It analyzes the enclosures of our time. People lost their homes and became strangers, as Rigoberta Menchú explains. In LA the people are migrants from El Salvador, Mexico, Nicaragua, and Guatemala; or from the other side of the Pacific—Cambodia, Vietnam, Korea, and the Philippines. They have been dislocated, dispossessed, displaced, dispensed with, disposed, disinherited, and dissed. That is the urban proletariat.

The Evil May Day riot of 1517 shows us the proletariat in motion, anticipating LA. In London workers obtained job security, health insurance, self-controlled education, and regulation of wages and hours. This was done with the guilds. Henry VIII brought Lombard bankers from Italy and merchants from France in order to undercut wages, lengthen hours, and break the guilds. This alliance between international finance, national capital, and military aristocracy was responsible for the imperialist nation-state.

According to *Hall's Chronicle* (1550) the young men of London would be revenged upon "the merchant strangers as well as on the artificer strangers." A secret rumor said the commonalty would rise on May Day. The king and lord mayor got frightened—householders were armed, a curfew was declared. Two guys didn't hear about it—they were arrested—the shout went out "prentyses and clubbes"—watermen, serving men, husbandmen mobilized seven hundred strong—the jails were opened—bricks, hot water, stones were thrown—a French capitalist's house was trashed. Then came the repression: cannons were fired into the city, three hundred were imprisoned, soldiers patrolled the streets, and a proclamation was made that no women should come together to "bable and talke, but all men should kepe their wyues in their houses." The prisoners were brought in through "ye stretes tyed in ropes, some men, some laddes, some children." Many were "adjuged to be hanged, drawen and quartered, and for execucion whereof, were set up 11 payre of galowes in diverse places." "This sight sore greued the people." The authorities "shewed no mercy, but extreme cruelty to the poore yongelinges in their execucion."

Thus the dreaded thanatocracy, or the regime of death, was inaugurated in answer to proletarian riot at the beginning of capitalism, just as perhaps towards its end the LA Uprising was an answer to the resumption after fifteen years in California of the death penalty when Richard Alton Harris was gassed a week earlier. The Evil May Day riots were X^2 caused by expropriation (people came to town having been dissed by enclosures) and by exploitation (people's jobs were dissed as the monarchy imported capital). Women with an alternative to patriarchal capitalism were burned at the stake as witches. Enclosure, conquest, famine, war, and plague ravaged the people who in losing their commons also lost a place to put a Maypole. In 1550 Parliament ordered the destruction of Maypoles. In 1644 the Puritans abolished May Day altogether. It wouldn't be observed in London for a long time, except as "a mere amusement for children," as it was said of the Ghost Dance after the Wounded Knee Massacre.

Although translators of the Bible were burned, its last book, Revelation, became an antiauthoritarian manual (influenced by hallucinogens, John of Patmos wrote it for slaves against the Roman Empire) useful to those who would turn the world upside down such as the Family of Love, the Anabaptists, the Diggers, the Levellers, the Ranters, and Thomas Morton, the man who in 1626 went to Merry Mount in Quincy, Massachusetts, and with his Indian friends put up the first Maypole in America. The Puritans destroyed it, exiled him, plagued the Indians, and hanged gays and Quakers. Morton was an immigrant, a boat person. So, a few years later, was Ann Lee, the Manchester proletarian, who founded the communal-living, gender-separated Shakers, who praised God in ecstatic dance. A cult, it might be said, like that in Waco, but unarmed.

Coming over on the *Mayflower* were the ancestors of Albert Parsons, the man as responsible for the modern May Day as anyone. Born in 1848 in Alabama, he was orphaned at five, and moved to Waco, Texas, where Aunt Esther, a slave, suckled him. Grown up, he fought for the Confederacy in the Lone Star Grays, then the McIngley Scouts. At war's end, his consciousness raised, he returned to Waco studying at Baylor and editing a radical reconstruction newspaper. The former slaves were hit with X^2. As Parsons said, "He was now a freeman without an inch of land, a cent of money, a stitch of clothes, or a morsel of food." Parsons led a prison escape attempt. He met Lucy, part Indian, part African American, and they married. The Ku Klux Klan was active in Waco (thirteen were lynched in April 1868) so the couple fled as political refugees to Chicago.

Albert became a typesetter, Lucy a seamstress. Both were active in the International Working People's Association, which called for 1) the destruction of existing class rule by energetic, relentless, revolutionary, international action, 2) a free society based upon cooperative production, and 3) equal rights for all regardless of sex or race. The slogans of the eight-hour movement are still useful: No Masters, No

Slaves! An Eye for an Eye! Vive la Commune! The Means of Life Belong to All! Liberty without Equality is a Lie! Agitate! Organize! Educate! Not to be a Slave is to Dare and Do! The Land for the Landless! The Tools to the Toilers! The Product to the Producers! One of their slogans went back to the biblical communism of the Peasants' Revolt of 1526—War to the Palace, Peace to the Cottage, Death to Luxurious Idleness.

Lucy worked with the homeless—"tramps" as they said in Chicago. She advised them, "Learn the use of explosives." She wrote the expropriated African Americans of Mississippi after a dozen had been lynched, "You are not absolutely defenseless. For the torch of the incendiary, which has been known to show murderers and tyrants the danger line, beyond which they may not venture with impunity, cannot be wrested from you." Expropriated from her land in Texas, exploited as a wage slave in Chicago, she was a turning point in American history X^2 and at the uprising of the urban proletariat which started the modern May Day.

Carolyn Ashbaugh sums it up in her book, *Lucy Parsons: American Revolutionary*:

> On May 1, 1886, the city of Chicago had been shut down in a general strike for the eight-hour working day—the first May Day. On May 4, the police broke up a meeting in Haymarket Square that had been called to protest police brutality. Someone threw a bomb, and the police began shooting wildly, fatally wounding at least seven demonstrators. Most of the police casualties resulted from their own guns. Eight radical leaders, including Albert Parsons, were brought to trial for the bombing .... The court ruled that although the defendants neither threw the bomb nor knew who threw the bomb, their speeches and writings prior to the bombing might have inspired some unknown

person to throw it and held them "accessories before the fact." All eight were convicted, and on November 11, 1887, Albert Parsons, August Spies, Adolph Fischer, and George Engel were hanged.

The death penalty against leaders of the exploited urban proletariat presaged massacre against a cult of the expropriated.

The UN has declared 1993 the year of the indigenous people. Lucy Parsons was such a person, unexpropriated. At the time of Haymarket, Geronimo and 35 men and boys and 101 women and children outwitted five thousand U.S. troops. Of course there were connections between the Indian and the workers' movements. A college man was secretary to the prophet and rebel Louis Riel, who proclaimed independence from the British Empire in Canada among the Métis Indians. Honoré Jaxon was his name, and when captured he escaped to Chicago in 1886 and wrote "Why We Fought; How We Fought; Why We Shall Fight Again." August Spies lived with the Chippewa Indians in Canada; for him communism wasn't a dream but a practical experience described in Lewis Henry Morgan's study of the Iroquois.

In 1883 Sitting Bull surrendered his rifle by his son to the United States: "This boy has now given it to you, and he wants to know how he is going to make a living." The boy went to Chicago, an indigenous proletarian. The Sioux were not finished, however, at the Pine Ridge and Rosebud Reservations. They began the Ghost Dance in a circle "with a large pine tree in the center, which was covered with strips of cloth of various colors, eagle feathers, stuffed birds, claws, and horns—all offerings to the Great Spirit." They didn't call it a Maypole and they danced for the unity of all Indians, the return of the dead, and the expulsion of the invaders on a particular day, the Fourth of July, but otherwise it might as well have been a May Day!

Wovoka, a Nevada Paiute, started it. Expropriated, he cut his hair. To buy watermelon he rode boxcars to work in the Oregon hop fields for small wages, exploited. The Puget Sound Indians had a new religion—they put the plug in the jug, they became entranced, they danced for five days, they jerked and twitched, they called for their land back—they were Shakers. Wovoka took this back to Nevada. "All Indians must dance, everywhere, keep on dancing." Soon they were. Porcupine took the dance across the Rockies to the Sioux. Red Cloud and Sitting Bull advanced the left foot following with the right, hardly lifting the feet from the ground. The federal agents banned the Ghost Dance! They claimed it was a cause of the last Sioux outbreak! On December 29, 1890, the U.S. Army (with Hotchkiss guns throwing fifty two-pound explosive shells per minute) massacred more than three hundred men, women, and children at Wounded Knee. As in the Waco holocaust, the Feds disclaimed responsibility. The Bureau of Ethnology sent out James Mooney to investigate. Amid Janet Reno–like tears, he wrote, "the Indians were responsible for the engagement."

May Day is sad: fifty-eight dead in LA, eighty-six dead in Waco, two thousand on death row. When will we stop it? Rodney King asked, "Can't we all get along?" the question proletarians ask each other from the beginning, since we are ruled by division. Some despair of an answer to the question and seek to escape the fate of X^2 by searching for "the end of all things" as did the Davidians. It was a Cheyenne ghost dancer who had the answer, "as the earth was too small for them and us, [the Great Spirit] would do away with heaven, and make the earth itself large enough to contain us all."

We have taken our walk in history; we avoided evasive jumps; we marched at Haymarket; we shuffled at Wounded Knee. We take strength from the million gay, lesbian, and straight people marching against AIDS. We take strength from the brothers and sisters coming from Haiti. We mourn Rosebud, Waco, and LA. We want justice! Down with expropriation! Away with exploitation. No X^2.

NO JUSTICE, NO PEACE

FOUR

A May Day Meditation

(2001)

Comrades and friends, May Day greetings! Here is "the day." The day we long to become a "journée," those days of the French Revolution when a throne would topple, the powerful would tumble, slavery be abolished, or the commons restored.

Meanwhile, we search for a demo for the day, or we gather daffodils and some "may" for our loved ones and the kitchen table. We greet strangers with a smile and "Happy May Day!" We think of comrades around the world, in Africa, India, Russia, Indonesia, Mexico, Hong Kong. With our comrades we remember recent victories, and we mutter against, and curse, our rulers. We take a few minutes to freshen up our knowledge of what happened there in Chicago in 1886 and 1887 before striding out into the fight of the day.

So during this moment of studying the day, I'm going to take a text from Friedrich Engels's *Socialism: Utopian and Scientific*, and I'll ask you to take it down from the top shelf of the spare room where you stuck it when Reagan came to power, or to go down into the basement and dig it out of a mildewed carton where you might have disdainfully put it during the Clinton years. Nowhere does Engels mention the slave trade. Nowhere does Engels mention the witch burnings. Nowhere does Engels mention the genocide of the indigenous peoples. He writes, "A durable reign of the bourgeoisie has been possible only in countries like America, where feudalism was unknown, and society at the very beginning started from a bourgeois basis."

Dearie me. Dear, dear, dear!

He has forgotten everything, it seems. He has swallowed hook, line, and sinker the whole schemata of: Savagery leads to Barbarism leads to Feudalism leads to Capitalism which, in turn, with a bit of luck, etc., will be transformed, down the line, in the future, when the times are ripe, etc., into socialism and communism. He has overlooked the struggle of the Indians, or the indigenous people, of the red, white, and black Indians. The fact is that commonism preceded capitalism on the North American continent, not feudalism. The genocide was so complete, the racism so effective, that there is not even a trace or relic of memory of the prior societies. So we fling him away as another Victorian European imperialist and white male, to boot.

But wait. Look again. Check out the essay at the back. He called it "The Mark." It's only a few pages. Perhaps you are misled by its German localism—its *Gehöferschaften* and its *Loosgüter*. The former term is the way the commoners of the Moselle Valley practiced the jubilee and the latter term is a land distribution system based on periodical assignments by lot. Engels is describing the commons of his neighborhoods. It is as substantial as Maria Mies in *The Subsistence Perspective*. You can smell the barnyard as you walk down the lane arm in arm to pick berries in the commons. Engels becomes a scholar of that "feudalism" which we thought he was discarding. But, no, in describing the pigs, the mushrooms, the turf, the wood, the unwritten customs, the mark regulations, the berries, the heaths, the forests, lakes, ponds, hunting grounds, fishing pools, he has quite forgotten his polemic against the economics professors (which is what inspired his tract) and he is relishing, shall we say, his very own indigenous self. I dare say he has had a few encuentros himself among the Germans. And we'll never forget that it was the criminalization of customary access to the commons which first drove Karl Marx to the study of political economy.

No, Engels is full of contradictions. I say get him back from the mildew and air out your copy. He has a political purpose. Engels is not that theorist we tossed off as hopelessly politically incorrect, and, taking all in all, a bad case for tenure. Part of his book he wrote for the professors of the SPD, but another part he wrote for the commoners and indigenous people—the peasants—who fled to the industrial towns. Moreover, he listened to them. They had lost their commons. Engels records the "traces," the "relics." These survive because of the French Revolution and the German one, which once again produced a free peasantry. "But how inferior is the position of our free peasant of today compared with the free member of the mark of the olden time! His homestead is generally much smaller, and the unpartitioned mark is reduced to a few very small and poor bits of communal forest. But, without the use of the mark, there can be no cattle for the small peasant; without cattle, no manure; without manure, no agriculture." That is the living commons. Engels knew of it. Engels is a free man; he knows that communism is possible. Engels is a revolutionary; he knows that it is not scheduled.

I say this not to rehabilitate Engels. I personally am less interested in him than I am in Tecumseh who refused to enter the house of Governor W.H. Harrison in August 1810 insisting on meeting in the open air. "The earth was the most proper place for the Indians, as they liked to repose upon the bosom of their mother." Having thus reposed himself, he asserted the society of the commons: "The way, the only way to stop this evil is for the red men to unite in claiming a common and equal right in the land, as it was at first, and should be now—for it was never divided, but belongs to all. No tribe has the right to sell, even to each other, much less to strangers.... Sell a country! Why not sell the air, the great sea, as well as the earth? Did not the Great Spirit make them all for the use of his children?"

But Engels had a global class politics; that is why we are interested in him again. What destroys the commons in Europe is what destroyed the commons of Tecumseh. Engels writes in 1880, "The whole of European agriculture, as carried on at the present time, is threatened by an over-powering rival, viz., the production of corn on a gigantic scale by America.... The whole of the European agricultural system is being beaten by American competition." It is true that Engels recognizes the commons in Germany but not in America. Having said that, Engels also recognizes that the preservation of the commons depends on an international struggle.

Now we return to May Day. What was responsible for that productivity of American corn? First, it was the fertility provided by a millennium of Native American corn culture on the common land (remember the mound makers who made thousands of tumuli, learn about the Hopewell people who brought corn from the Maya one thousand years ago, visit the fabulous serpent mound of Ohio during your summer travels). Second, it was the members of the Moulders Local 23 at the McCormick mechanical reapers' works of Chicago who went on strike for the eight-hour day in 1867 and whose struggle directly resulted in the Haymarket demo of 1886. And then the hangings.

So, now as they gather in Seattle and Windsor and Prague and Brazil and Quebec, precisely to sell the air, the water, the earth, we pose the common alternative, under many names, untheorized and common, oh! how so very, very common, common to the slaves, common to the indigenous peoples, common to the women, common to the workers. Here is the light and the heat of the day. I shall miss you, dearest comrades, at the launchings in New York and Boston of the *Auroras of the Zapatistas*.

FIVE

May Day at Kut and Kienthal

(2003)

Inasmuch as the historian's craft depends on written records, then the answer to the question posed in the title of V. Gordon Childe's classic book about the Tigris and Euphrates, *What Happened in History?* is well answered in the title of another classic book on the same subject by Samuel Kramer, *History Begins at Sumer*, because that's where writing began. With the American "liberation" of Iraq and the subsequent destruction of the library of Baghdad and its museum of antiquities, we could say, therefore, that history while not quite coming to an end has become impossible to write. But there are other sources of knowledge of the past, such as song and story, flora and fauna, with which we'll have to make do, not to mention what we remember. Baghdad scholarship survived the sacking by Genghis Khan and there is no reason to think that it will not persist after the burning of the books by the United States.

Still… following the planetary mobilizations of February 15 and March 22, on the one hand, and this barbaric devastation of Iraq on the other, we don't feel exactly like dancing around the Maypole. We need that history which seizes hold of "a memory as it flashes up in a moment of danger." While the storm from paradise blows us into the future, the angel of history turns its face to the past, commemorating, remembering: May Day and the Haymarket hangings; May Day and the eight-hour day struggle; the May Days of *soixante-huit*; May Day and the struggles against apartheid; May Day and the Central American solidarity movement. We do not smile.

Every May Day story has its point, and Rosa Luxemburg expresses ours: "The brilliant basic idea of May Day is the autonomous, immediate stepping forward of the proletarian masses, the political mass action of the millions of workers," she wrote on the eve of the Great War, and wasn't it so just last month, March 22, and the month before, February 15, when we millions around the planet autonomously stepped forward? And why did we autonomously step forward? Peace in Iraq. Yet Red Rosa said, "The direct, international mass manifestation: the strike [was] a demonstration and means of struggle for the eight-hour day, world peace, and socialism." Peace, yes; but we left aside the eight-hour day and socialism. Is that why we failed to stop the war?

While the Americans are wrapping the cradle of civilization in its winding sheet, the angel of history stops at May Day 1916 and the terrible siege, surrender, and slaughter at Kut on the Tigris River. We shall contrast it with the Kienthal Manifesto issued on May Day 1916 with its prophecy of proletarian parturition. First, Kut; then Kienthal.

KUT. In the spring of 1916 at Verdun two million men were engaged in massive mutual holocaust; there were 676,000 losses. In Mesopotamia, tens and scores of thousands of sepoys of the Indian Expeditionary Force D, on behalf of the British Empire, disembarked at Basra at the beginning of the war, with the strategic objectives of: 1) securing the oil supply from Persia, 2) protecting the main corridor to India, and 3) preventing a jihad combining Arab, Afghan, with a rising in India. We could sum it up, as Connolly did: "the capitalist class of Great Britain, the meanest, most unscrupulous governing class in all history, is out for plunder." A fourth objective emerged on the sly. British government in India wished to annex Mesopotamia, but British Empire in London preferred to operate from its lair in Cairo rather than Delhi.

The lure of Baghdad proved irresistible to General Townshend, the commander. Foolishly (for the Persian refineries were already secured) he led the renamed Mesopotamian Expeditionary Force up the Tigris River, extending his lines of communication far beyond the powers of his base to supply it with food. Repulsed before reaching Baghdad, he was forced to retreat a hundred miles to Kut. There followed a four-month siege, a humiliating defeat, and surrender on the eve of May 1, 1916. Parallel with this narrative of disaster ran two subplots, a) the soldiers' resistance, and b) the orientalizing derring-do of Lawrence of Arabia and the charming wiles of Gertrude Bell.

a) Townshend found keeping up morale "the most difficult of all military operations" and one in which the British soldier is "very prone to get out of hand." They arrived and dug in at Kut after two days of forced marches, and then suffered heat, exhaustion, floods, disease, famine. The Indian battalions had practically become "armed bands." The bulk of the troops were Muslim. Seditious pamphlets in Urdu and in Hindustani called on the troops to rise and murder their officers, and join their bothers the Turks, who would pay them better and provide grants of land. One sepoy did attempt to shoot his officer, several deserted, and twelve to fourteen soldiers cut off their trigger fingers. Many were from Punjab. Dysentery claimed fifteen dead a day, and twenty from starvation. Townshend complained about the "transborder Pathans." He wanted them returned to India. They refused to eat horseflesh, and though he mixed Hindu and Mohammedan on picket duty and outpost work, he could not break their solidarity. Altogether, seventy-two deserted.

Moberly, whose three volumes on the Mesopotamian campaign provide the official history, explained: since the Pathans were without private property, the British promise to assure rightful succession to their property in the event of their being killed was without effect! Behind this logic were imperial fears of mutiny and commonism. Against these, terror was the traditional remedy. The Arab inhabitants of Kut would not sell their food. Townshend asked headquarters for gold, and explained, "I could not flog 6,000 people into taking paper money. All I could do was to keep them in good behaviour by shooting one now and then *pour encourager les autres* when spies, etc., were caught."

b) Gertrude Bell was the first woman to win a First in Modern History at Oxford. Her grandfather was a rich British industrialist, supplying one third of British iron. She danced, she rode horses, she spoke Arabic, quoted Milton, archaeologically discovered cities, charmed imperious egos. She became the silken agent of English guile. Gertrude Bell wrote from Military Intelligence's Arab Bureau, next to the Cairo Savoy, "It's great fun." In Cairo Lawrence intrigued to encourage the Arab revolt against the Ottoman Empire. Gertrude Bell was dispatched to India. The disaster at Kut put a decided damper on its ambitions. "I hate war; oh, and I'm so weary of it—of war, of life," she sighed from Basra, in March 1916 during the frightful heat. That was the month that the British government began to pay Sharif Hussein £125,000 gold sovereigns a month, a deal she helped set up.

Gertrude dallied with Lawrence, "We have had great talks and made vast schemes for the government of the universe. He goes up river tomorrow, where the battle is raging these days." A month after the surrender, indeed, the Arab revolt began. Lawrence was able to write a scathing report on the Indian Army's operations in Mesopotamia. The English political officer "Cox is entirely ignorant of Arab societies," plotted Lawrence. An obstacle to the Arab revolt—Indian ambitions for the cradle of civilization—had been discredited. "The most important thing of all . . . will be cash," quoth his instructions. In April Lawrence was authorized to offer the Turks £1,000,000 to quit the siege of Kut; though he doubled it, Khalil Pasha rejected it scornfully.

In March Lawrence read Coleridge, *The Rime of the Ancient Mariner*; several parallels may be made—the thirst ("Water, water, everywhere/Nor any drop to drink"), the sun, the heat, the loneliness, the guilt of the mariner for his responsibility in the wanton murder of the crew. What sights had Lawrence seen in Kut? Who were the starving and wasting men? The English were from Dorsetshire and Norfolk, depressed agricultural counties, hardy specimens of the English proletariat whose experience was depression. There were Punjabis, Pathans. The Inland Water Transport Service employed in its Mesopotamian contingents men from the British West Indies Regiment, the Nigerian Marine Regiment, the West African Regiment, the Coloured Section, the Egyptian Labour Corps. Lawrence saw starve the motley international of an imperialist army.

> The many men, so beautiful!
> And they all dead did lie:
> And a thousand thousand slimy things
> Lived on; and so did I.

Lawrence, clearly, would have his limitations as an imperial servant: in his master's view empire was not slime, despite the fact that it was oil they craved!

a) February 1916 finds Gandhi speaking in Karachi. Having returned to India the year before he vowed to be silent for a year, and only recently had he begun to speak out.

Truth and fearlessness were his themes, as only they could remove the demoralizing atmosphere of sycophancy and falsity. However, these salutary results required not-spitting. Self-restraint was the necessary condition to national liberation, he taught, "when we conquer our so-called conquerors." Earlier that month, however, despite not-spitting, he created a furious row with a speech at Benares Hindu University. "It is necessary that our hearts have got to be touched and that our hands and feet have got to be moved"—the doctrine of *satyagraha* was activist or nothing. "In her impatience India has produced an army of anarchists," he continued. "I myself am an anarchist but of another type." He contrasted himself to the anarchist terrorists responsible for the bombing campaign which before the war had annulled the British partition of Bengal. "I honor the anarchist for his love of country. I honor him for his bravery in being willing to die for his country; but I ask him: Is killing honorable?" Just as the argument in front of the students was promising to get interesting, Miss Annie Besant, the English liberal, interrupted, "Please stop it." Later she explained she had noticed the CID taking notes, "I meant to do him a kindness and prevent the more violent interruption which would probably have taken place, had I remained silent." More slime.

b) Gandhi may have overlapped with Gertrude Bell in Karachi, but where Gandhi derived nourishment from the people, she pitied them: "Swollen with wind and the rank mists we draw" is the phrase she remembers in April from Milton's *Lycidas*. It is from a passage about corruption between leaders and led which begins with . . . what, the slime of Wolf Blitzer from the desert? A Pentagon briefing? Ari Fleischer?

> What recks it them? What need they? They are sped;
> And when they list, their lean and flashy songs

Grate on their scrannel pipes of wretched straw;
The hungry sheep look up, and are not fed,
But swoln with wind, and the rank mist they draw,
Rot inwardly, and foul contagion spread;
Besides what the grim wolf with privy paw
Daily devours apace, and nothing said.

Not a glimmer of proletarian creativity could allay the view of people as sheep. Milton at any rate went in dialogue with the Levellers and Diggers of his day, while Gertrude Bell used Milton as another code of ruling-class mutual recognition.

a) She did not draw the parallel to the experience which the surgeon at Kut remembered, namely, that the cats became bolder as food became scarcer, and they began "with privy paw" to lurk about the windows and doorways of the surgery. Major Barber, the English sawbones, was not pleased by his first impression of Kut, "Approaching from the east, almost the first thing that caught the eye was a gibbet." He spent days with stretcher-bearers, bhisties, and women water drawers. The soldiers called the place "Messypot," he tells us. Nighttime shelling they called "the hate." He cursed war and the economic necessities that bring it about. Famine advanced. Then came the slaughter of the beasts—a thousand horses, mules, camels, all except the officers' chargers, and Townshend's dog whose daily walk counted among Barber's duties. He composed a menu, reflecting the *class* of the rank and file.

Potage aux Os de Cheval
Sauterelles Sautés
Starlings en Canapé
Filet de mule
Entrecote de Chameau

For Major Barber May Day 1916 was the arrival of the hospital ship with jam, swag, and bubbly.

On April 29, after a siege of four and a half months, General Townshend lowered the Union Jack and burned it. Twenty-three thousand soldiers had been killed in four futile attempts to relieve the siege; then on the eve of May Day thirteen thousand were taken prisoner. "It was one of the great mistakes in British military history," writes Barker in *The Neglected War: Mesopotamia, 1914–1918.* The prisoners? Captain Shakeshaft observed them ragged, barefooted, dying of dysentery. "One saw British soldiers dying with a green ooze issuing from their lips, their mouths fixed open, in and out of which flies walked." Many were contracted to railway construction for a German company working in Turkey. Altogether the British Empire lost forty thousand casualties, concludes Moberly.

b) If in America the capacity to inflict terror in Iraq while simultaneously denying it is called Liberation, in England it goes by The Stiff Upper Lip. Gertrude Bell and General Townshend didn't let the side down. Despite having had her black silk gown rifled by pilfering hands at the Delhi P.O., she cheerfully wrote referring to the mulberries and blossoming pomegranates, "Even Basra has a burst of glory in April." As for General Townshend, he concluded the terms of surrender with this: "Finally, I asked Khalil Pacha to send my faithful fox terrier 'Spot' down to the British force to my friend Sir Wilfred Peek, so that he might reach home. He was with me in the Battles of Kurna, he was at Ctespiphon and in the retreat, and he killed many cats during the defense of Kut. He reached England safely, and I met him on my return to my home in Norfolk."

Gertrude Bell would become known as "the uncrowned queen of Iraq," after the British took Baghdad in February 1917. She wrote in words that could come from Ms. Robin Raphel, slated to run the Iraq trade ministry, or Ms. Barbara Bodine, awaiting her assignment in Wolfie of Arabia's Iraq, "We shall, I trust, make it a great centre of Arab civilization, a prosperity; that will be my job partly, I hope, and I never lose sight of it." James Connolly explained on St. Patrick's Day 1916, "The essential meanness of the British Empire is that it robs under the pretence of being generous, and it enslaves under pretence of liberating." Hence, the flash song of liberation grates on the scrannel pipes of wretched straw which we know are there not to sing songs but to suck up you-know-what.

a) In "Mesopotamia—1917" Rudyard Kipling wet his whistle, cleared his throat of anything that might grate, and definitely raised his voice to express grief and a very healthy specific—class hatred:

> They shall not return to us, the resolute, the young,
>> The eager and whole-hearted whom we gave:
> But the men who left them thriftily to die in their own dung,
>> Shall they come with years and honour to the grave?
>
> Shall we only threaten and be angry for an hour?
>> When the storm is ended shall we find
> How softly but how swiftly they have sidled back to power
>> By their favor and contrivance of their kind?

Mercifully, Kipling leaves God out of it. Plus, he demands justice, not oil, to compensate for the sacrifice of the young. Kipling told one half of the story. The other half remains to be told. Is it too late for the Subaltern Studies historians to recover the oral tradition of the POWs who fled, deserted, and escaped from Kut? Some people were ready to answer Kipling's two questions. This brings us to the second half of our essay.

KIENTHAL. They met in Switzerland, a center of internationalism (financial, artistic, and revolutionary) but unconnected by internet or al-Jazeera or Robert Fisk, with the disasters between the Tigris and Euphrates. Their remedy for war and famine, which only anticapitalist revolutionaries can provide, was offered up from the Alpine village of Kienthal. Two such different ecologies, different elevations, different temperatures, different flora and fauna as Kut and Kienthal would be hard to imagine, yet as human communities both in 1916 retained links with a nonindustrial commons—the marsh Arabs on their reeds and islands in the former, the booleying of the high pastures in the latter. The previous September anti-imperialist socialists had secretly and bravely met at Zimmerwald. The work of such intrepid souls as Lenin and Rosa Luxemburg resulted in the Kienthal Manifesto of May Day 1916. The manifesto was preceded by debate and discussion.

Rosa Luxemburg published her *Junius Pamphlet* in the spring of 1916, as if with Bechtel Corporation and Baghdad in mind. "Business is flourishing upon the ruins. Cities are turned to rubble, whole countries into deserts, villages into cemeteries, whole populations into beggars . . . thus stands bourgeois society . . . as a roaring beast, as an orgy of anarchy, as a pestilential breath, devastating culture and humanity." As for the proletariat, "No pre-established schema, no ritual that holds good at all times, shows it the path that it must travel. Historical experience is its only teacher; its Via Dolorosa to self-liberation is covered not only with immeasurable suffering, but with countless mistakes."

None were bitterer than she over the betrayal of July 1914 when the so-called representatives of the European international proletariat voted with their national belligerents, sending millions of fellow workers to slaughter one another. She noted that socialism is "the first popular movement in world history that has set as its goal, and is ordained by history, to establish a conscious sense in the social life of man, a definite plan, and thus, free will." But it does not fall like manna from heaven. She posed a choice: "either the triumph of imperialism and the destruction of all culture and, as in ancient Rome, depopulation, desolation, degeneration, a vast cemetery. Or, the victory of socialism, that is, the conscious struggle of the international proletariat against imperialism and its method: war." Amid the slaughter of Verdun and the starvation of Kut, she returned to an axiom of history: human beings make it, the conscious historical action by conscious historical will. They did not pretend that peace was patriotic or that they could win without struggle.

Lenin gave a speech in Switzerland in February 1916. He quoted the *Appeal to Reason* of September 11, 1915. Eugene Debs said, "I am not a capitalist soldier; I am a proletarian revolutionist. I do not belong to the regular army of the plutocracy, but to the irregular army of the people. I refuse to obey any command to fight from the ruling class. . . . I am opposed to every war but one; I am for that war with heart and soul, and this is the worldwide war of the social revolution. In that war I am prepared to fight in any way the ruling class may make necessary." Gloden Dallas and Douglas Gill, in *The Unknown Army: Mutinies in the British Army in World War I*, write that a year later, also on September 11, the English recruits in France mutinously demonstrated. In Mesopotamia the soldiers organized themselves to return home, when ordered up country against the local population. One of the veterans remembered, "We refused saying that we had not enlisted for this purpose & as there was always trouble there, we should have had difficulty in getting back. We stood our ground & gained the day."

Lenin welcomed *The Junius Pamphlet*, although he argued the necessity of wars of national liberation. In Zürich during the spring of 1916 Lenin wrote *Imperialism, the Highest Stage of Capitalism*, which would be used in the anticolonial struggles of the twentieth century—China, India, Kenya, Algeria, Vietnam. He studied the growth of monopolies and cartels; he studied finance capital: "It spreads its net over all countries of the world." He observed its dynamics: 1) "the more capitalism is developed . . . the more desperate the struggle for raw materials," or 2) "imperialism is, in general, a striving towards violence and reaction." He explained how the proletariat drew rank mist and became swollen with wind. Superprofits from plundering colonies enabled the metropolitan working classes to become opportunist and susceptible to nationalist appeals, permitting the betrayal of the trade unions and socialist parties. "It has grown ripe, overripe, and rotten," Lenin wrote. He noted its two fundamental weaknesses, a) it bribed its lower class into acquiescence, and b) its armies were recruited from subject peoples.

Lenin lived around the corner from the Cabaret Voltaire where the artists and musicians in the spring of 1916 thought up the name Dada for an art to cure the madness of the age. Ed Sanders in volume one of his beautiful *America: A History in Verse* described an evening there:

—a holy, mind-freeing rinse of nonsense
  to laugh away
           the stench of the trench
              a Rinse heard as far away as
                    San Francisco

If theirs was the rinse, Lenin gave the scrubbing. Lenin quoted Cecil Rhodes, "If you want to avoid civil war, you must become imperialists." This precisely was the pivot point: how to turn imperialist war into civil war. Here was the transition from defense to offense. Rosa Luxemburg too argued against the siege mentality in favor of armed, free people on'a move. You study Lenin and Luxemburg in that year and you do not find sectarian bitterness or the irreconcilable differences of gender antagonism. Among the many things Luxemburg and Lenin agreed on that year was denunciation of the Social Democrats for refusing to intercede on behalf of a comrade in the Cameroons who faced a death sentence for organizing an uprising against the war. These are comrades denouncing war, condemning betrayal of the official opposition, analyzing imperialism, praising the creativity of the working class, and they search the world to find it.

From these discussions came the Kienthal May Day Manifesto of 1916. If Kut describes a progenitor of our problem, then Kienthal describes a solution. Its words apply to us. Addressed to workers of town and country, "You have only the right to starve and to keep silent. You face the chains of the state of siege, the fetters of censorship, and the stale air of the dungeon. . . . They try to incite you to betray your class duty and tear out of your heart your greatest strength, your hope of socialism."

"The governments, the imperialist cliques, and their press tell you that it is necessary to hold out in order to free the oppressed nations. Of all the methods of deception that have been used in this war, this is the crudest. For some, the real aim of this universal slaughter is to maintain what they have seized over the centuries and conquered in many wars. Others want to divide up the world over again, in order to increase their possessions. They want to annex new territories, tear whole peoples apart and degrade them to the status of common serfs and slaves."

"Courage! Remember that you are the majority and that if you so desire the power can be yours." By May 1916 W.E.B. Du Bois and James Connolly had found the desire and the courage. It consisted of a) defense against terrorism and b) offense against imperialism.

Du Bois had recently written that "Africa is the prime cause of this terrible overturning of civilization," world war. He wrote, "The white working man has been asked to share the spoil of exploiting 'chinks and niggers.'" Having invaded Haiti, Santo Domingo, Mexico, and Nicaragua, the United States grew rank with terror and racism. Marcus Garvey of Jamaica arrived in New York in the spring of 1916, asking Du Bois to chair his meeting. Du Bois called for a revolution, "Democracy in determining income is the next inevitable step to democracy in political power." When the Easter rebels were called fools, Du Bois appealed to the heavens, "Would to God some of us had sense enough to be fools!" May Day at Du Bois's *The Crisis* was entirely occupied in the struggle against lynching. It inveighed against the terrorism in the United States. The April issue was against the lynching of six men in Georgia, while the next issue, on "The Waco Horror," reproduced the most searing photographs of the century, the charred stumps of mutilated, burned, and hanged Texas proletarians.

James Connolly reiterated, "A Rich Man's War and a Poor Man's Fight!" He discovered the war profiteers. He analyzed the economic incentives for joining up (employment + cash for women who sent their husbands to war). He berated the union bureaucrats and praised the Dublin dockers and London seamen. He recalled British robbery of Irish common lands, and in that stroke of genius which operates by observing the obvious he noted that "the spirit of adventure" must be counted a revolutionary force. He doubted that the political leprosy of militarism could be excised without the red tide of war. Opportunities are for those who seize them, and so, on to Easter.

The rule of insurrection is audacity, audacity, audacity! So, despite the capture on Sunday of Roger Casement and the loss of the arms he was shipping from Germany, the Easter Rising commenced anyway on Monday, April 24, 1916, asserting the right of the men and women of Ireland to its ownership, in the oft-reprinted proclamation. Scattered in buildings about the town the insurgents communicated with one another by means of bicyclists. Though crushed in less than a week, its reverberations thrilled the oppressed from Jamaica to Bengal. In Dublin Connie Markievicz was second in command at Stephen's Green. To her disappointment she was spared execution owing to her gender, and instead awakened on May Day in her cell at Kilmainham Gaol to the sound of rifle reports as her comrades were executed by firing squad. They removed her to prison in England where she amused the bread-and-water gang by extensively reciting from *The Inferno*, as well as her own words:

> Dead hearts, dead dreams, dead days of ecstasy,
> Can you not live again?
> Nay, for we never died . . .

Joe Hill, the songwriter, was shot on November 19, 1915. James Larkin came over from Dublin for the funeral, where they sang Hill's popular "The Rebel Girl":

> There are women of many descriptions
> In this queer world, as everyone knows,
> Some are living in beautiful mansions,
> And are wearing the finest of clothes.
> These are blue-blooded queens and princesses
> Who have charms made of diamonds and pearls:
> But the only and Thoroughbred Lady
> Is the Rebel Girl.

The proletarian revolution is not the restoration of matriarchy, though it definitely entails the defeat of patriarchy and *Hausfrauisizerung* (to use the phrase of Maria Mies). And we can easily understand, given the leadership of the women of the planet on the great days of February 15 and

March 22, that the term *proletarian*, etymologically speaking, meant the women or breeders of empire, but who were now taking steps to realize our planetary power as a class.

We have looked back with the angel of history—at the low siege, surrender, and slaughter at Kut, and at the high Alpine manifesto of proletarian internationalism of Kienthal—and still the wind blows us into the future, which the ruins of the libraries of Baghdad and the bleeding of funds for the municipal libraries in the United States have not yet destroyed, for we take the treasures with us. The coincidences of May Day (Kut and Kienthal) like the coincidences of September 11 (mutiny and terror) are not magic, though they need to be discovered; they arise merely from probabilities. May Day is one day in 365. September 11 is another rotation of the planet. As the earth rotates prior to our revolution, these are the constants: imperialism and the struggle against it, capitalism and the struggle against it, capital punishment and the struggle against it. Meanwhile, against the slime, Gandhi said clean up your act. Against the flash song, Lenin offered economic analysis. Against terror, Du Bois offered unflinching truth. Against the swollen wind and rank mist of patriotism, Red Rosa offered the International. Against all the odds, James Connolly offered audacity. Against defeat, Joe Hill offered laughter.

We learn from Franklin Rosemont's magnificent *Joe Hill: The IWW & the Making of a Revolutionary Workingclass Counterculture* that the cremated ashes of Joe Hill were put in envelopes and sent to every IWW local in every country of the world—Latin America, Asia, Africa, Europe—and were released to the breezes on May Day 1916. For the followers of the sky-gods, Jahweh and Allah, we laugh with Joe Hill,

> You will eat, bye and bye,
> In that glorious land above the sky;

Work and pray, live on hay,
You'll get pie in the sky when you die.

As for the dirt-gods, Mammon and Moloch, not having mopped them up, we have not yet earned our laugh.

SIX

Magna Carta and May Day

(2005)

Magna Carta and May Day: What have they to do with each other? First of all let's recollect what we know about each of them. Magna Carta (meaning *large charter*) put an end to a civil war between King John and the English barons 790 years ago this June. So, while we might think of it in the framework of political science as a constitution, it also contained something of the nature of a treaty.

The barons opposed King John for many reasons. We are most familiar with the complaints which were redressed in chapter 39 of the Charter, the "nullus liber homo" clause, "No free man shall be taken, or imprisoned, or disseised, or be outlawed, or exiled, or any otherwise destroyed, nor will we condemn him but by lawful judgment of his peers, and by the law of the land." The words are familiar to us from the Fifth and Fourteenth Amendments to the U.S. Constitution.

The chapter has been frequently quoted during the last year because the U.S. government—let us call it the chain of command—has violated the provisions that derive from this chapter—the prohibition of torture, habeas corpus, trial by jury, and due process of law. Those who oppose the despotism and lawlessness of "the chain of command" refer to Magna Carta because it is part of the heritage of mankind against the bullying, cruelty, and greed of kings, potentates, and "sovereign powers." These are protections for the individual. But what of our class?

Now turning to May Day we recollect it as a workers' holiday because the Federation of Organized Trade and Labor Unions of the United States and Canada "resolved that eight hours shall constitute a legal day's labor from and after May 1, 1886." In Chicago the iron molders at the McCormick Works were locked out even though McCormick himself was enjoying a profit rate of 71 percent, which he enhanced by cutting wages by 15 percent. The iron molders protested, and the police shot four of them dead.

A few days later thousands of people attended a meeting near Haymarket Square to hear several speakers protest. When the crowd began to dwindle away a stick of dynamite was thrown during the police charge. All hell broke loose, many were killed, and the sheriff of Cook County instructed the police to "make the raids first and look up the law afterwards," expressing a pre–Magna Carta view of authority. Eight men were brought to trial eventually, and four of them were hanged, Albert Parsons, George Engel, Adolf Fischer, and August Spies whose last words were these: "There will come a time when our silence will be more powerful than the voices you strangle today."

The time that August Spies anticipated came soon, and the voice for an eight-hour day was soon heard beyond the United States and Canada to the whole world, as workers, peasants, students celebrated May Day and with it, to quote Oscar Ameringer, "the divine message of more money and less work." That "divine message" is actually a faith-based initiative if there ever was one. But it has been lost in those modern forms of enslavement, debt peonage, forced labor in penitentiaries, export zone sweatshops, mandatory overtime, multiple job holding, and feminization of poverty, which, even if we are not all comfortable calling it the work of Satan, certainly characterizes contemporary planetary labor. For if the eight-hour day actually came as a result of May Day struggles, it surely has long since gone.

So, that's what most of us know about Magna Carta and May Day. And what they have in common is loss—the lost liberties, the lost eight-hour day. They seem to have little to do with each other, separated by thousands of miles and hundreds of years. Even if we put aside geography and chronology for a moment and compared them on the basis of class struggle, it is the difference that seems to stand out. The feudal barons who stood up against King John were themselves large landed magnates, latifundista, who commanded the labor of serfs and villains in the feudal mode of production. The struggle in Chicago in contrast was a class struggle between industrialists and the proletariat, a new type of ruling class even though we dub them robber barons, and a new type of worker, huddled in slums and crammed into factories.

It is true that Magna Carta contained provisions to benefit or to protect Jews, city dwellers, and merchants, acknowledging in these commercial interests a new historical force, a force which was relatively weak at the time, yet its inclusion signified that Magna Carta attempted to weld together a class bloc, or coalition, providing to the disparate elements methods of dispute settlement, policy making, and overarching spiritual supremacy of the Christian church.

Magna Carta was a treaty in the class war, and it helped to make a ruling class. As for King John, as soon as he could, he resumed war and discarded Magna Carta but then he dropped dead. The story of his death became the stuff of legend among the peasant commoners conveyed by word of mouth and remembered as oral history even by William Morris who in breathing its bold and blunt heroism

I paraphrase. Fleeing his enemies King John lost all his baggage in an onrushing tide of the sea, and in a foul mood took shelter in Swinestead Abbey, Lincolnshire. "How much is this loaf sold for?" he asked at dinner, and when told one penny he answered, "by God, if I live for one year such a loaf shall be sold for twelve pence!"

One of the monks nearby heard this and considered that his hour and time to die had come, and that it would be a good deed to slay so cruel a king and so evil a lord. So he went into the garden and plucked plums and replaced the pits with venom. Then he came before the king and knelt saying, "Sire, by St. Austin, this is the fruit of our garden." The king looked evilly on him and said, "Eat first, monk!" So the monk ate but changed not countenance any whit. So the king ate too. Presently right before the king's eyes the monk swelled and turned blue and fell down and died. Then waxed the king sick at heart, and he also swelled, sickened, and died.

This is history from below, and like any history it must be examined. First, plums, not thought of as native to England, did indeed originate in Byzantium and probably came to England at the time of Magna Carta with the returning crusaders. But whether this delicious weapon of the spiritual suicide bomber actually came from Palestine, as St. George, England's patron saint, most certainly did, has not yet been determined with certainty by English botanists. I intend to suggest that the story of Magna Carta can never be understood without at the same time considering the manifold influences of Islam even upon that grey and cold island that lies off the coast of northwestern Europe.

Second, not only were the herbariums and orchards of the English monasteries early examples of collective labor, they were also progenitors of communal living upon natural resources held in common. Thus, when the monk offered King John, who in his own infinite greed had attempted to gather unto his own self all the forests of England, a fruit of the garden, it was a fruit in the double sense of both a product of human labor and a product of the earth, rain and sunshine, as the peasants who told this story and as William Morris who repeated it well understood. We however, sunk in the slough of alienation, must be reminded.

Let us return to May Day. When George Rawick, the historian of the oral history and self-activity of the Afro-American struggle against slavery, came to the University of Massachusetts on May Day to help us observe the hundredth anniversary of Haymarket, he wanted to emphasize not that Albert Parsons partnered up with Lucy Parsons, herself an Afro-American, for multiculturalism is easy to grasp. Rawick emphasized the surprising and odious fact that Albert Parsons had risked his life once for the slave masters of the Confederacy! Rawick wanted to emphasize that human beings change owing to circumstances, owing to one another. We do not change just as we please; it takes agitation, education, organization.

The troops in Chicago were seasoned in fighting against the Sioux Indians who had defeated Custer. Black Elk referred to "the story of all life that is holy and is good to tell, and of us two-leggeds sharing in it with the four-leggeds and the wings of the air and all green things; for these are children of one mother and their father is one spirit." Yes, the Indian wars of the Great Plains were wars of privatization. Frank Cushing lived five years among the Pueblo Indians and reported, just a few years before Haymarket, of "the old women who have been off among the mountains gathering peaches all day, staggering home at sunset, under huge baskets, strapped across their foreheads, full of the most delicious fruit."

I mention peaches only because I mentioned plums. Mmm. The fruits have no nations, though it is true their germplasm is endangered by enclosures. My point is that privatization has smashed a huge variety of commoning regimes around the world and its police have massacred a huge number of commoners.

After King John died, the Charter of Liberties was brought out again but this time with a significant revision and a significant addition. The addition was the smaller Charter of the Forest in contrast to which Magna Carta got its name. The Charter of the Forest certainly was not a "communist manifesto," however it was most certainly a charter for the commons because it sought to return not the whole forest to the people, but some of the customary rights to its resources to the practise of commoning. These included pannage, or the right to put pigs into the forest to dine on the acorns, beechnuts, and mast, thus helping to provide the two-leggeds with food for the winter. Another common right recognized in the Charter of the Forest was herbage, or permitting cows to graze in forest lands and purlieus, thus providing if not "roast beef of olde Englande" then the children with milk. Chiminage, or the right to travel in the forest without having to pay tolls, was also acknowledged, a form, we might say, of public transport.

In addition to these additions to the Charter of Liberties, the Magna Carta itself was revised in its chapter 7, which made provision that the widow "shall have her reasonable estovers in the commons." Estovers referred to wood gathered in the forest for the distinct purposes of 1) fuel for warmth and cooking, 2) handles for implements and tools, and 3) timbers for fencing and building. The "reasonable estovers to the commons" thus refers to what we call today social security and the safety net. These provisions were gender specific not because women were particularly defenseless against the male-dominated structures of economic and legal power—the call for gender equality which rang out from southern France among the Albigensians was heard all over Europe—but because women played a leading part in the commonages and in the remembrance of commoning practices. And here they are in Magna Carta!

Albert Parsons said this at his trial. "What is socialism or anarchism? Briefly stated it is the right of the toilers to the free and equal use of the tools of production and the right of the producers to their product." Now we are in a position to come to some conclusions. We can see what Magna Carta and May Day have in common. Parsons does not refer to estovers, pannage, herbage, chiminage, and so forth. He raises the slogan of socialism or anarchism, not feudalism. Parsons intends to include men as well as women in socialism. Parsons refers not just to the material civilization that depended on the forest. He intends to include the factories and forges fueled by coal. Parsons intends in his meaning to include all toilers, not just the hands at any moment gripping the plough.

Magna Carta and we must remember the defenses against the "chain of command." Magna Carta and we must remember to make a coalition of alliances, our movement of movements. Magna Carta and we must remember our commons, our earthly treasury. May Day and the eight-hour day. May Day and worldwide working-class solidarity. May Day with William Morris:

> And in hope every spring-tide come gather together
> That unto the Earth ye may tell all your tale.

SEVEN

May Day with Heart

(2006)

The moon and hours have revolved again, dear hearts, and May Day is upon us. Spring has sprung as usual, though a strike, a boycott, a holiday, a refusal—call it what you will—looms hopefully on Monday morrow, and that is unusual. We'll wear white in solidarity with the immigrant worker against rampant criminalization, against the universal miserablism, the broken levees, the constant enclosures, great walls, razor-wired borders, burning frontiers, and the castrametation of the planet by the USA (as the Romans called the science of military base construction).

I asked Massimo De Angelis, a family man, who went up to Gleneagles last year to protest against the G8, what to say on May Day. He replied, as is his wont, as if he were a hobgoblin sitting on a mushroom. He likes the mushroom because it is nocturnal, it may cause dreams, and many of the fungi are not yet privatized. As for the hobgoblin it is a country figure of tricks and mischief against the masters. Plus, I know he likes Helen MacFarlane's translation of *The Communist Manifesto*, "A frightful hobgoblin stalks throughout Europe."

"Well," the hobgoblin said to me, says he, "whatever you say, say it with heart."

Very well, but James Green, the splendid labor historian, says that after the terrible events in Chicago beginning on May Day 1886, Americans suffered "a loss of heart." The labor historian tells us we have lost precisely what the hobgoblin asks us to find.

How are we to resolve this dilemma? This year the answer must come from the South. Eduardo Galeano, the historian from Uruguay, reminds us of a simple etymology, that the word *record*, as in the record of the past, derives from Latin, to pass again through the heart (*cordis*).

We cannot avoid the ache of history; its grief we feel in the gut. In preparation for the May Day general strike (will it be general?) by the undocumented workers we organize our banners (and Maypoles?), prepare our slogans (open borders, troops home, no enclosures, health care for all), hopefully many will try their hand at a manifesto, and we alert our lawyer friends to prepare defense for the inevitable victims. It is also essential to study our past, and to learn about our May Day. We must study the record. It must pass through our heart again.

So we take down the classics from the shelf or make sure our local library has them at hand: Martin Duberman's fine novel on Haymarket, Roediger and Rosemont's timeless scrapbook, the late Paul Avrich's stirring monograph, or the old CP classic on May Day by Philip Foner. To these we now add James Green's just-published *Death in the Haymarket: A Story of Chicago, the First Labor Movement, and the Bombing that Divided Gilded Age America.* Go get it! We need it for Monday and every May Day thereafter. The book is trying to put some freedom back into history telling us that it could have been otherwise. We call this human agency. The theory is something like this. It's human history, we're humans, history is something we make with our deeds and words. This is where free will rubs up against determinism. As soon as you put class into the theory it begins to make sense: the ruling class is determined to exploit us, so naturally it says that it can't help it—the steam hammer is stronger than John Henry, you can't stand in the way of progress, and so on. That's the determinism. On the other hand, the working class will be free. We are not cogs in a wheel; we have not forgotten the good old wooden shoe. We do have choices. We will (for instance) wear a white T-shirt on May Day. Human agency thus resolves itself into the struggle between the classes.

It never took any multicultural brilliance to discern that the actual fundaments of the USA are threefold:

a) it was robbed from the indigenous peoples,

b) its swamps were drained, forests felled, and fields prepared by African slaves, and

c) the railroads, factories, mills, and mines were built and run by immigrants from Europe and Asia.

The ruling class from Madison on forward knew its duty to keep these three, if not fighting one another, then separated. Thus, radical reconstruction came to an end in 1877 in New Orleans beginning that period of Afro-American history called "the Nadir"; the Plains Indians were destroyed in 1877, taking the death of Crazy Horse for a symbol of the destruction, and the third, in a word, death at Haymarket.

The Cuban poet José Martí lived in exile in New York at the time and wrote brilliantly on the Haymarket martyrs. Although "the disagreements and rivalries of the races already arguing about supremacy in this part of the continent, might have stood in the way of the immediate formation of a formidable labor party with identical methods and purposes, the common denominator of pain has accelerated the concerted action of all who suffer." Here is heart as a political principle.

James Green recovers forgotten dreams, that one, for instance, which tied Abraham Lincoln to the cooperative commonwealth. The great sacrifices included the death of Lincoln whose funeral catafalque came through tens of thousands of mourners in Chicago on May Day 1865, amid a light drizzle of rain. America could become a cooperative commonwealth instead of a competitive camp of capitalism. William Sylvis, Andrew Cameron, and Ira Steward maintained continuity in the north after the Civil War. William Sylvis rebuilt the Molders' Union with foundry workers at the farm reaper works of McCormick. They were the industrial vanguard by 1865. Andrew Cameron was a Scottish Chartist and an editor in Chicago of the *Workingman's Advocate* whose idea was that production should be for use, not profit. Ira Steward, an abolitionist and machinist from Massachusetts, established the Eight-Hour Leagues in 1866, on May 2 of that year in Chicago. A year later the first eight-hour law took effect on May Day, passed by the Illinois legislature and signed by Richard Oglesby, governor and friend of Abraham Lincoln, the rail-splitter. QED.

What happened in 1886? The context was this. The imperialists had divided up Africa the year before. "Accumulating mansions and factories on the one hand, and wretched masses of people on the other" is how Martí painted the background. Otherwise, the founding of the American Federation of Labor by the cigar maker Samuel Gompers, riots in Seattle against Chinese laborers, the capture of Geronimo, the gold rush to Witwatersrand in South Africa, Gottlieb Daimler perfected the internal combustion engine, *Das Kapital* was published in English, the French Impressionist pointillist canvas *A Sunday Afternoon on the Island of La Grande Jatte* was designed and displayed to erase thoroughly the visual memories of the Paris Commune and *la semaine sanglante*.

Despite the boom and bust of the trade cycle, despite unemployment, union workers "began to anticipate their own emancipation from the endless workday and growing tyranny of wage labor." The Noble and Holy Order of the

Knights of Labor, they called themselves, mystical and with a moral code of chivalry and generous manhood. The motto of the Knights was "One for All, and All for One." From squalor they proposed nobility. An 1877 circular read, "Working men of Chicago! Have you no rights? No ambition? No Manhood? Will you remain disunited while your masters rob you of your rights and the fruits of your labor? For the sake of our wives and children and our own self-respect, LET US WAIT NO LONGER! ORGANIZE AT ONCE!"

The freight handlers struck, the upholsterers struck, the lumber shovers went on strike. Four hundred seamstresses left work in joyous mood. A storm of strikes swept Chicago, on the first of May 1886. The great refusal, Jim Green calls it. It was a new kind of labor movement that "pulled in immigrants and common laborers." Irish, Bohemian, German, French, Czech, Scot, English, to name a few. In Socialist Sunday Schools, brass bands, choirs, little theatres, saloons, there was a working-class culture in Chicago. The *Chicago Tribune* (May 6, 1886) hated it and compared the immigrants to zoological nightmares. It demanded deportation of "ungrateful hyenas" or "slavic wolves" and "wild beasts" and the Bohemian women who "acted like tigresses."

In the spring of 1886 strikes appeared everywhere in industrial centers; called the Great Upheaval, it agitated for shorter hours. Of course they were against the mechanization of labor, against the exploitation of child labor, opposed to the convict lease system of labor, and opposed to contract labor. The anthem of the Knights of Labor was the "Eight-Hour Song,"

> We want to feel the sunshine;
> We want to smell the flowers;
> We're sure God has willed it.
> And we mean to have eight hours.

We're summoning our forces from
Shipyard, shop and mill;
Eight hours for work, eight hours for rest,
Eight hours for what we will.

Sam Fielden joined the International Working People's Association in 1884 after fifteen years hauling stone and digging ditches. His father was a Lancashire handloom weaver and a ten-hour man. Sam was a Methodist.

Thanksgiving Day of 1884 they had a poor people's march and Parsons quoted from James (the brother of Jesus?) chapter 5,

Next a word to you who have great possessions. Weep and wail over the miserable fate descending on you. Your riches have rotted; your fine clothes are moth-eaten; your silver and gold have rusted away, and the very rust will be evidence against you and consume your flesh like fire. You have piled up wealth in an age that is near its close. The wages you never paid to the men who mowed your fields are loud against you, and the outcry of the reapers has reached the ears of the Lord of Hosts. You have lived on earth in wanton luxury, fattening yourselves like cattle and the day for slaughter has come. You have condemned the innocent and murdered him; he offers no resistance.

What a remarkable prophecy! The Sioux Wars removed the people of the Plains, the U.S. Cavalry thundered up and down, murdering Indians, and lathering the land with blood, while the mechanical reaper shaved the grasses. When historians speak of "the open frontier," it means the Indians were wiped out. This is the genocide which led to the agricultural depression in Europe, produced by the mechanical reaper scalping the prairie. No, the reapers were not paid.

Fast Food Nation perhaps may not yet have been up to speed yet the starting gun had been fired. Swift and Armour were the big meatpackers: they organized the mechanization of death, the machines of mass slaughter of cattle and swine. The Union Stock Yards had just been constructed. The employers threatened to employ "the whole machinery of government," including the army, "to enforce the laws of the market." Mechanization indeed was taking command.

On May Day 1886 as the workers of the United States struck for the eight-hour day, the police shot and killed four strikers at the McCormick Works. August Spies issued the flyer, calling the workers to rise, to arms, for revenge. On May 4 strikes resumed, now joined by union switchmen, laundry girls, even students from some of the schools.

At the Haymarket, tons of hay and bushels of vegetables were brought in from the Dutch truck farms. Transportation was by horsepower. Indeed, then horses were part of the working class, as Jason Hribal has provoked us to thinking. Haymarket in Chicago in May 1886 was like Guernica in Spain in 1937 when the Condor Legion wiped it out by bombing: that is to say it was a busy, crowded market, ideal for terrorism.

The weather changed, the moonlit sky suddenly turned dark, as a cloud blew over, just preceding the blast. The police advanced. A bomb was thrown. In the mêlée a large number of police were wounded by friendly fire from their own revolvers. Sam Fielden was shot in the leg. Henry Spies took a bullet for his brother. Seven policemen fell. But who threw the bomb? John Swinton, the most influential labor journalist in the land, argued that the police themselves provoked the violence to stop the strike movement for the eight-hour day.

A period of police terrorism ensued. There were hundreds of arrests. There were raids at meeting halls, saloons, and newspaper offices. Captain Schaack put suspects into the sweatbox (a small pitch-dark wooden container) for hours to make them talk. Albert Parsons fled to Mexico, it was rumored, or was "hiding out among the negroes." That summer there was a trial, conducted by passion, judged by bigotry. Green tells the story with verve and drama. Witnesses were paid off. The jury consisted of salesmen, clerks, a high school principal, well-off all.

Nina Van Zandt, the handsome Vassar graduate and heiress, made eyes at August Spies during the trial. In the jailhouse, the love affair developed. Spies told the court, "Here you will tread upon a spark, but here, and there, and behind you and in front of you, and everywhere, flames will blaze up. It is a subterranean fire. You cannot put it out. The ground is on fire upon which you stand."

Michael Schwab defended anarchy saying it was the antithesis of violence. Parsons charged the court with "judicial murder." He explained socialism and anarchism. "I am doomed by you to suffer an ignominious death because I am an outspoken enemy of coercion, of privilege, of force, of authority. Your every word and act are recorded. You are being weighed in the balance. The people are conscious of your power—your stolen power. I, a working man, stand here and to your face, in your stronghold of oppression, denounce your crimes against humanity." Neebe was found guilty and punished with fifteen years in the penitentiary. Louis Lingg killed himself. Fielden and Schwab had their sentences commuted to life imprisonment. Albert Parsons refused alcohol. He sang "La Marseillaise" and songs by Bobbie Burns. August Spies became the newspaper editor of the *Arbeiter Zeitung* in 1884. Before his execution, Spies had said, "The day will come when our silence will be more powerful than the voices you are throttling today."

We are finding voice. Cindy Sheehan gives us voice. "Si se puede" gives us voice. The Chicago idea was this: trade unions could take mass action against capital and the state. This idea has been disappeared or throttled. The magical realism of the ruling class proclaims May Day to be Law Day (had they not heard of "Ozymandias," or "Humpty Dumpty"?). None died from a broken neck, all strangled to death, slowly as it appeared to the witnesses, convulsing and twisting on the rope.

That was November 11, 1887.

James Green tells us that it was a turning point in American history. The killing at the McCormick plant, the bombing at Haymarket, the court proceedings, and the hanging of November 11 extinguished the Knights of Labor, defeated the eight-hour movement, suppressed the radicals. The Mary Magdalene, so to speak, of the suffering proletariat was Lucy Parsons, widow of Albert, daughter of Mexico. She bore witness to subsequent generations, touching Mother Jones, Big Bill Haywood, Emma Goldman, Clarence Darrow, Eugene Debs, with the principles of *los mártires*. Henry Demarest Lloyd was silenced, then wrote *Wealth Against Commonwealth*, the exposé of John D. Rockefeller's Standard Oil Company, the first of the muckrakers.

Beneath the concameration of the Great Hall at Cooper Union in New York City, Samuel Gompers of the new American Federation of Labor appealed against the death sentence. Instead: fifty years of industrial violence, and when workers, especially immigrants, found themselves at war with their employers: the courts, the police, the armed forces. These laid the "bone deep grudges" which Nelson Algren wrote about. James Green concludes, "We are today living with the legacy of those long-ago events."

The 151-foot Statue of Liberty was dedicated only two weeks before the hangings in Chicago. Inscribed on its pedestal were the words of Emma Lazarus:

> Give me your tired, your poor, Your huddled masses, yearning to breathe free, The wretched refuse of your

teeming shore. Send these, the homeless, tempest-tossed, to me: I lift my lamp beside the golden door.

John Pemberton, a pharmacist, invented a medicine to relieve headaches and alleviate nausea. It combines coca leaves from the Andes with cola nuts from Africa, mixed with water, caramel, and sugar: Coca-Cola, the Atlantic remedy for the ills of the barbarism of capitalism.

Both William Morris in England and José Martí exiled from Cuba in Manhattan likened the Chicago working class to a cornered animal.

William Morris wrote a death march for the funeral of Alfred Linnell, the young man killed by the London police after the November 13, 1887, Trafalgar Square meeting and demonstration. It was two days after the hanging at Haymarket. Alfred Linnell, lo!, will come knocking at the gate, unbidden, insistent, calm, upright. The Harold Pinter moment.

> What cometh here from west to east awending?
> And who are these, the marchers stern and slow?
> We bear the message that the rich are sending
> Aback to those who bade them wake and know.
> Not one, not one, nor thousands must they slay,
> But one and all if they would dusk the day.
>
> We asked them for a life of toilsome earning,
> They bade us bide their leisure for our bread;
> We craved to speak to tell our woeful learning:
> We come back speechless, bearing back our dead.
> Not one, not one, nor thousands must they slay,
> But one and all if they would dusk the day.
>
> They will not learn; they have no ears to hearken.

They turn their faces from the eyes of fate;
Their gay-lit halls shut out the skies and darken.

But, lo! This dead man knocking at the gate
Not one, not one, nor thousands must they slay,
But one and all if they would dusk the day.

He took it to the street: one week he is beaten up at
Trafalgar Square, another week a poor law clerk is murdered
by police at Trafalgar Square, and a third time in the streets,
to sing this lament. This is heart. With his bids and bides
and bades, with the awending and the woefuls, the man is
searching for some kind of language that has endurance,
that is beneath the radar, off the grid, and might be recognized by hobgoblins and coyotes.

Morris serialized *The Dream of John Ball* between
November 1886 and January 1887. The dates give us the clue:
the Haymarket trials had passed. The revolutionary attempt
in Chicago had been preempted. The Chicago idea had failed,
temporarily at least. In these circumstances Morris dove
deep to middle ages, and ranged far, to Afro-America. In
that way he maintained his revolutionary commitment. He
imagines victory! "To dusk the day" means to win. "They"
refers to the police, employers, capitalists, and ruling class.
Eloquence arises from silence. He was reading aloud on the
same day his own *Dream of John Ball* and B'rer Rabbit. He is
looking for a people's story told in the people's language
with the people's future: the opposite of the official story, not
at all the evasions of institutional prose or the commands of
cogitation machines.

Prince Kropotkin at the Sunday lecture supper at the
Hammersmith socialist hall told the fable of the Russians
and the Redskins. He told this story rather than commit
himself, one way or the other, to the quarrelsome socialists

and anarchists. The African American slave selects a hero, "the weakest and most harmless of animals," Br'er Rabbit of course, "and brings him out victorious in contests with the bear, the wolf, and the fox." Not malice triumphs but mischievousness.

In 1887 Lord Acton wrote, "Power tends to corrupt and absolute power corrupts absolutely." U.S. wheat prices fell to sixty-seven cents a bushel, England ate bread from grains of North American plains, indirect consequences of the defeat of the Plains Indians and the McCormick workers. Jim Crow law passed in Florida requiring racial segregation among railway passengers.

Pablo Neruda, José Martí, even Walt Whitman had a big, hemispheric conception of America: two continents, half the planet, yet united by the German geographer Humboldt's Afro-America, a big S: New Orleans, Cuba, Venezuela, and Brazil. What happens in one part affects the other: sugar, aluminum, gold, bananas, silver, copper, coffee, rum, pot, and coke, yes, they are the products, the commodities, ripped from the bowels of the earth. They're easier to recognize than the undergrounds of people, whose migrations, sailings, tunneling have preserved the memory of *los mártires*.

José Martí predicted that "the world's working class will revive them [memories of the Haymarket martyrs] every First of May." "That is still not known, but Martí always writes as if hearing, where it is least expected, the cry of a newborn child," wrote Galeano.

In Havana in 1887 the anarcho-syndicalists started a newspaper, *El Productor*, which covered the Haymarket tragedy. In 1890 they prepared a May Day manifesto calling on Cubans to support the international demonstration for the eight-hour day. The workers responded with a unified, musical parade. Speeches called for equal rights between blacks and whites and called for the unity of all workers. The authors of the May Day manifesto were arrested and brought to trial. Their acquittal was greeted by a huge demo.

May Day was celebrated in Mexico in 1913. From then on Primero de Mayo became a national holiday known as the Day of the Martyrs of Chicago in Italy, France, Spain, Argentina, Cuba, Mexico. In 1903 Teddy Roosevelt signed an immigration law denying entry into the United States of anarchists, paupers, prostitutes, and the insane.

Galeano celebrated the marriage of heart and mind. "From the moment we enter school or church, education chops us into pieces: it teaches us to divorce soul from body and mind from heart. The fishermen of the Colombian coast must be learned doctors of ethics and morality, for they invented the word sentipensante, feeling-thinking, to define language that speaks the truth."

In Milan on the first international May Day (1890) a correspondent wrote, "On this day laborers all over the world should feel the unity of their class as a bond superior to all others." Is it possible to make such a solidarity? Can heart be so large? On May Day 1894 Coxey's Army of the Commonweal arrived in Washington to lobby for the unemployed, only to be arrested and imprisoned for walking on the grass. The IWW, or Wobblies, printed thousands of stickers, reading: "I Won't Work More Than 8 Hours After May 1st 1912. How About You?"

On May Day 1917, all Petrograd was en fete as the *New York Times* reported and business was at a complete standstill. In Germany meanwhile the Spartacus group leafleted, "Women workers! Male workers! The last groans of our thousands of murdered brothers and sons, the sobs of the wasted women and children call us forcibly and imperiously to the red worker's May 1st demonstration, with the gleaming words: down with the war! Up with people's brotherliness!" At the Metropolitan Opera House in New York City on May

Day 1925 garment workers raised their voices to sing "The Internationale." Congress mandated the eight-hour day in the Fair Labor Standards Act. From 1886 to 1938 = fifty-two years. In May Day of that year a march on the South Side of Chicago was led by a float featuring a hooded man. In one direction of time, August Spies; in another direction of time, Abu Ghraib.

Galeano visited Chicago but his exploration of Haymarket was fruitless, instead he found an old poster at a bookstore displaying the African proverb, "Until the lions have their own historians, histories of the hunt will glorify the hunter." The hunter had put in 1889 a statue of a policeman at Haymarket. The Weathermen blew up the police monument on October 6, 1969, and then again in 1970.

The urbanicide of Katrina, the castrametation of Iraq, the devaluation of the working class, the absolute rule of the petrolarchs have produced gut-wrenching grief and sorrow. Our head spins and spins in the dizzy search for cause and effect, searching the origin of this twisted, agonizing karma.

Halfway between the gut and the head lies the heart. The heart and soul of our movement may be found on May Day, and it's going to take our arms and legs to find them, as well as our brains. So let us join the hobgoblin.

Take heart with *Death in the Haymarket* in hand!

All out for May Day!

Bibliography

Algren, Nelson. *Chicago: City on the Make.* 1951. Reprint, Chicago: University of Chicago Press, 2001.

Avrich, Paul. *The Haymarket Tragedy.* Princeton: Princeton University Press, 1984.

De Angelis, Massimo. www.thecommoner.org.uk.

Duberman, Martin. *Haymarket: A Novel.* New York: Seven Stories Press, 2003.

Foner, Philip. *May Day: A Short History of the International Workers' Holiday, 1886–1986*. New York: International Publishers, 1986.

Galeano, Eduardo. *Memory of Fire*, Vol. 2, *Faces and Masks*. Translated by Cedric Belfrage. London: Quartet, 1987.

Galeano, Eduardo. *The Book of Embraces*. Translated by Cedric Belfrage and Mark Schafer. New York: W.W. Norton, 1991.

Green, James. *Death in the Haymarket: A Story of Chicago, the First Labor Movement and the Bombing That Divided Gilded Age America*. New York: Pantheon Books, 2006.

Harris, Joel Chandler Harris. *Uncle Remus: His Songs and Sayings*. New York: Appleton, 1880.

Logan, Rayford W. *The Negro in American Life and Thought: The Nadir, 1877–1901*. New York: Dial Press, 1954.

MacCarthy, Fiona. *William Morris: A Life for Our Time*. New York: Knopf, 1995.

Shnookal, Deborah, and Mirta Muñiz, eds. *José Martí Reader: Writings on the Americas*. New York: Ocean Press, 1999.

Roediger, David, and Franklin Rosemont. *Haymarket Scrapbook*. Chicago: Charles H. Kerr, 1986.

Thompson, E.P. *William Morris: Romantic to Revolutionary*. 1955. Reprint, Oakland: PM Press, 2011.

EIGHT

Obama May Day

(2010)

In Ann Arbor, Michigan, you can observe in the movement the desire to bring the troops home from Iraq and Afghanistan and the other six hundred overseas military bases, the release of political prisoners, the establishment of a commons at the library lot, opposition to the racism in Benton Harbor, freedom for Palestine, support (rather than dismissals) of school teachers, opposition to the proliferation of asphalt parking lots in favor of gardening and bicycles, more trees (remembering the name of our burg), and support for the upcoming Detroit Social Forum. A loose network here called "Bringing It Back, Taking It Forward" has helped to revive our movement.

More and more of us understand that war and the banking scandal, sickness and home foreclosures are symptoms of a civilization that is finished, yet neither the Christian militia nor the Tea Party is our bag. The scholars among us lament the closure of the Shaman Drum, a great bookstore, and we ruefully note that an excellent English language bookstore flourishes in Oaxaca, Mexico. Who is "backward" now?

Alan Haber was a founder of Students for a Democratic Society fifty years ago here in Ann Arbor, and nowadays he directs the Megiddo Project, which seeks to replace the God of Battles with peaceful conversation at a round table he has built. He asked me to sketch out a short May Day pamphlet bringing together, first, the history of May Day, second, a celebration of the jubilee or the fiftieth anniversary of both SDS and the Student Nonviolent Coordinating Committee (SNCC), and third, an invitation to Barack Obama who is to speak on May Day at the Michigan football stadium to join the immigrant rights march in the afternoon in Detroit. No problem, I ventured to Alan, considering the history of May Day. How are we to bring together the three forces for social change—students, immigrants, and political presidential power? To begin with we need a methodology.

Our first methodological principle starts with Aneurin Bevan, the Welsh coal miner who went on to install the national health system in Britain. He would remind himself, and everyone else, not to forget that everything starts "at the point of the pick." This was in the days before the continuous miner when coal was hewed, even "crafted" he said, from the underground coal face. The energy of industrialization began there. The methodological principle puts the worker at the center of history, and the coal miner at the center of the industrial working class.

We need a symbol of reproduction, and Vandana Shiva, the feminist advocate of India, can suggest one, for she issued the international warning against the taking of the seeds from the women and thus their power. "The seed, for the farmer, is not merely the source of future plants and food; it is the storage place of culture and history." The bowl of seeds had to be hidden against the "scientific" agronomists who were in the pay of Monsanto or other international genetic engineers ("the knights of the gene snatchers," quips Alan). The invisible work of reproduction surrounds history. The commons, often invisible and generally in the care of women, is the second methodological principle.

So (the hammer and the sickle having had their day), let us proceed in our methodology on the basis of "the point of the pick" and "the seeds in the bowl." Because the pick takes things apart, it may act as a metaphor for analysis, and because the bowl holds stuff together it may stand for synthesis. If the pick be analysis and the economics of production, it thrives in the realm of the inanimate. If the bowl be synthesis and social reproduction, its realm is the animate. These are both crucial operations of historical thinking. Consider the history of May Day.

Merry Mount

In North America it began with immigrants, the English immigrants to Massachusetts, and they were of two minds. The gloomy Puritans wanted to isolate themselves ("the city on the hill") and having accepted hospitality of the native people either made them sick or went to war against them. Thomas Morton, on the other hand, arriving in 1624, wanted to work, trade, and enjoy life together with the natives. He envisioned life based on abundance rather than scarcity. Three years later he celebrated May Day with a giant Maypole, "a goodly pine tree of eighty feet long was reared up, with a pair of buckhorns nailed on somewhat near unto the top of it."

William Bradford, coming over on the *Mayflower*, landed at Plymouth Rock. He thought Indians were instruments of Antichrist. Of Thomas Morton and his crew, he wrote, "They also set up a maypole, drinking and dancing about it many days together, inviting the Indian women for their consorts, dancing and frisking together like so many fairies, or furies, rather; and worse practices. [It was] as if they had anew revived the celebrated the feats of the Roman goddess Flora, or the beastly practices of the mad Bacchanalians."

Because Morton taught the Indians how to use firearms, the Puritan Myles Standish attacked and destroyed this early rainbow gathering. Morton was twice deported by the Puritans, and twice exonerated in England. He died in Maine.

Bradford gets one thing right. May Day is very old, and nearly universal (in one form or another). It is a festival of planting, of fertility, of germination. It is a community rite of social reproduction. Years later Nathaniel Hawthorne bemoaned this road not taken. Not taken yet, we might add. The circular bowl of seeds symbolizes the day in several senses. Picking away at time we easily find the commons.

Haymarket

From Merry Mount (1627) to Haymarket (1886), two and half centuries passed. An empire diminished (England 1776), a nation was founded, bankers established themselves, slavery advanced, an army and a navy manifested "destiny." With the pick of analysis we take up with the coal miners, the railroad builders, the ditch diggers. With the bowl of synthesis we apprehend how all together make a force in history. As a force it includes the commons, the space of autonomy, independent of capital and privatization.

In 1886, the ironworkers of the Molder's Union struck at the McCormick Works in Chicago, setting in motion the events that led to the infamous Haymarket bombing, the hanging of four workers, and our modern May Day. Let's pick it apart. First, these workers struck for an eight-hour day. This had been at the center of the post-Civil War movement of industrial workers:

> We want to feel the sunshine;
> We want to smell the flowers
> We're sure God has willed it.
> And we mean to have eight hours.
> We're summoning our forces from
> Shipyard, shop and mill;

Eight hours for work, eight hours for rest.
Eight hours for what we will.

Second, many of them were Irish immigrants and as such brought knowledge of the Famine and knowledge of the struggle by the Molly Maguires in the anthracite fields of Pennsylvania the decade earlier. They remembered the Day of the Rope (June 1877), the first of a series of more than twenty hangings against the Irish coal miners of Pennsylvania.

Third, in Chicago the workers were making a machine to reap the grasses, the grains of the North American prairies. The machine presupposed the robbery of lands from the indigenous people—the Lakota, the Comanche, the Apache, the Metis in Canada—this is the fourth point of analysis. Its so-called productivity would result in a) the globalization of food as both grain and meat passed through Chicago and the Great Lakes into the hungry bellies of Europe, and b) the shortsighted agriculture which would result in the disastrous Dust Bowl two generations hence. Chicago was a hub of world food organization as well as a forward base in the conquest of the common lands of the prairies.

The strike was suppressed by soldiers and a worker was killed. The class-conscious workers of Chicago protested. Irish and Poles, socialists and anarchists, Catholics and communards, former Blues (Yankees) and former Grays (Confederates) joined in a howl of outrage. Albert Parsons, the former Confederate soldier whose consciousness was awakened by the Civil War to join forces with the former slaves and present wage slaves (marrying Lucy Parsons, part African American, part Native American), summarized the Haymarket gathering: "We assembled as representatives of the disinherited."

Truly, in one way or another the immigrants had been dispossessed, not only from their present means of production (capital), but from their past subsistence (commons) in the lands of their origins. Furthermore, the soldiers attacking the Chicago workers had learned how to kill in the Indian wars and to expropriate the indigenous peoples from their communal systems. This was the era when the critique of capitalism was elaborated by many hands. Few at the time swung the pick with greater point than Karl Marx who, unlike pure theorists, asked the workers what they thought in an inquiry of more than a hundred questions. This was to become the essence of subsequent student movements.

At Haymarket in Chicago, a stick of dynamite was thrown into the crowd (did the police do it? was it the deed of an anarchist or socialist activist?) and all hell broke loose. A spectacular and terrible trial was held, unfair in every respect, and Sam Fielden, August Spies, Albert Parsons, Oscar Neebe, Michael Schwab, Adolph Fischer, George Engel, and Louis Lingg were found guilty. On November 11, 1887, despite an international campaign, four of them were hanged, preparing the way for the Gilded Age of American capitalism.

Chicago has never been the same, nor has the world labor movement: on the one hand, Chicago became the center of brutish capitalism, led by gangsters such as Al Capone, on the other hand a multiethnic working class arose from Mississippi, Mexico, Poland, or Ireland and writers such as Carl Sandburg, Nelson Algren, or Richard Wright told us about it. The "Chicago Idea," the notion that revolutionary unionism can combine militant union with mass action, is not quite dead. In remembrance of *los mártires* May Day became the worldwide day of the workers and the eight-hour day.

The pick (the workers) and the bowl (the commons) must take us to the jubilee of SDS and SNCC. But the path is not direct. The coal miners had to overcome the ethnic and language civilizations deliberately instilled by the bosses. The United Mine Workers of America was formed in 1890. Mother Jones was born on May Day 1838 in county Cork, Ireland. In 1901, she was in Pennsylvania urging the wives of the miners to form a militia wielding brooms and banging pots and pans. The prosecutor called her "the most dangerous woman in America." In 1905, in Chicago, she helped found the Wobblies, the IWW, or Industrial Workers of the World, whose preamble stated: "The working class and the employing class have nothing in common. There can be no peace so long as hunger and want are found among millions of working people and the few, who make up the employing class, have all the good things of life." Mother Jones herself urged us "to pray for the dead and fight like hell for the living."

Common lands were not within their program. Yet the commons (of land and labor) became an anticapitalist dream. The rulers will try to establish control over reproduction with walls, fences, ICE, terror, detention. The rulers will do so by population policy, controlling birth rates and death rates, eugenics, family allowance, maternity leave, abortion, and what John Ruskin called "illth" or the opposite of health and wealth alike. The rulers attempt to organize the structures of labor markets, the skill sets and levels by education and immigration policies. In American history, slaughter and disease are weapons against the indigenous; slavery and immigration are weapons against workers. In fact terror has always been the instrument against the commons.

I believe in its early agreements with the bosses that, in addition to his own birthday, the coal miner's mother's and mother-in-law's birthdays were paid days off. It indicates that a community of women backed up the miners. Oscar Ameringer, an immigrant often called "the Mark Twain of American socialism," wrote for the miners' union in Illinois under the pseudonym of Adam Coaldigger. He acknowledged that the miner had access to the commons, hunting and fishing, yet he couldn't do both at once, mine all day and half the night and then go hunt and fish! It was the coal miners who backed the union organizing during the Great Depression.

The epic, the decisive, event of the twentieth century (at least one of them) was the Bolshevik Revolution in Russia of 1917. The Cold War of the United States against the USSR seemed to occupy the ideas, the institutions, and the politics of the world. (The United States went so far as to shift the workers' holiday to the beginning of September, pretending that May Day was a Russian holiday!)

After the Russian Revolution, communism was interpreted as a matter of state or government, far, far removed from actual commoning experiences, which were dismissed as belonging to either a "primitive social formation" or "backward," "undeveloped" economies. This began to change in 1955 as the second great theme of the twentieth century—the national liberation struggles of colonies from European empires—congealed on the world stage. These two themes—the communist revolution and the national liberation struggles—provide essential background for the birth of SNCC and SDS.

Again, let us take up the pick and the bowl.

Indonesia

In 1955, a group of Asian and African nations met in Indonesia. They were seeking a third way, neither communist nor capitalist, aligned with neither the USSR nor the United States. Chou En-lai, Nehru, Nasser, and Sukarno were some of the leaders present. This movement of ex-colonies developed the block of nonaligned nations in 1960 that met in Belgrade.

Led by Sukarno, Nehru, and Tito, the attempt on the one hand was to find a third way between socialism and capitalism during the Cold War impasse, and on the other hand it was to assert the independence of the Third World liberation forces. In either case these independent entities were results of that liberation, Yugoslavia after World War I, India and Indonesia after World War II.

Richard Wright was the writer who understood racism, the working class, and Chicago. He was born in 1908 in Mississippi, the grandchild of slaves. He moved to Chicago and joined the Communist Party. His 1940 photo essay of the workers in the American South was an eloquent visual preliminary to the civil rights movement of the Rosa Parks generation and the Montgomery bus boycott. In 1940, too, he composed *Native Son*, the unparalleled study of male proletarian rage in a racist society. In the Sixties, however, Third Worldism was the American optic of internationalism. It was deliberately and self-consciously revolutionary in its rejection of the USA.

Richard Wright was present at Bandung, Indonesia, in 1955 and wrote a book about it, *The Color Curtain*. It was the first meeting of the Third World countries, neither capitalist nor communist. He saw it as a meeting of "the despised, the insulted, the hurt, the dispossessed—in short, the underdogs of the human race were meeting." Of the American newsmen he met, "they had no philosophy of history with which to understand Bandung." He prepared himself for the trip by devising a questionnaire and using it as a basis of conversation with fellow travelers on trains and planes (seventy-eight of these questions are included in *The Color Curtain*): Were you educated by missionaries? What do you think of capital punishment? Is it ever justifiable to use the atomic bomb? Do national inferiority feelings find expression in your country? Do you want to see your country industrialized? Do you think that a classless society, in an economic sense, is possible? Here again is the empirical pick at work: the student asks questions, the student interrogates her subject, and then listens.

"With us land has always been communal," replied one Indonesian. Not one of the Asians he spoke to defended "that most sacred of all Western values: property." An Indonesian man summed up the recent history of his country, "Now the common people are not getting benefits from that revolution. That's why today we are threatened with another revolution."

Ninety percent of the land in the outer islands was under shifting cultivation or swidden agriculture; they had no notion of private property in land, and production was not for commerce. High biodiversity is maintained, with very high nutrient content stored in soil and in the biotica. The swidden plot is not a "field" but a miniature forest. By contrast Java and inner Indonesia under rice cultivation or *sawah* depends on terraces and elaborate irrigation systems carrying water, algae, and nitrogen. Seeds from nurseries instead of broadcast. The 1870 Agrarian Land Law proclaimed that "waste" land was government property. It inaugurated the corporate plantation. Pepper, rubber, and coffee were produced on the planation for export. Village lands were preempted. The involution of life, the ranking system, and evisceration of village rights followed. In the 1950s, local peasants took over roughly half the plantations but made dense, vague, and dispirited communities.

Pramoedya Ananta Toer (1924–2006), the Indonesian novelist of Dutch imperialism, was imprisoned on Buru Island between 1965 and 1979. He describes life there in *The Mute's Soliloquy*, "But the Buru interior was not empty; there were native people living off that piece of earth long before the arrival of the political prisoners forced them to leave their land and huts behind. Then, as the prisoners converted the savanna into fields, the native people watched their hunting grounds shrink in size. Even the area's original place names were stolen from them and they too were calling the area 'Unit 10.'" He was lucky I suppose, because perhaps one million, certainly several hundred thousand, Indonesians were massacred between 1965 and 1966. Henry Kissinger and the CIA were complicit in this mass slaughter.

Kenya

In 1952, the indigenous movement for independence from the British Empire began in Kenya. Guerrilla forces in the forests attacked the imperialists on the plantations. They formed the Land and Freedom Army, but the British called them Mau Mau, and the name stuck. The colonials ruling Kenya adopted the Swynnerton Plan in 1954, a massive land grab.

Cash cropping and land titling destroyed traditional communal economies in favor of a system based on commodity production. It effectively led to the confiscation of lands and "the consolidation and enclosure." Moreover the terracing of lands forced labor to make coffee plantations. Public grazing lands were closed. "One no longer feared to push aside traditional customs." Women and children suffered most. Women's entitlement to communal lands disappeared. A million men and women were forced into detention centers and concentration camps. Part of the notorious British campaign against the Land Freedom Army, or Mau Mau, was against a background of mass hangings and concentration camps. Male leaders failed to articulate a position in favor of women's access to land. Kenya attained independence in 1963.

The experience of Mau Mau is partly described in Ngugi wa Thiong'o's *Weep Not Child* (1964) and *A Grain of Wheat* (1967). In Detroit, February 14, 1965, Malcolm X explained that the Mau Mau frightened the white man throughout the colonial world. The FBI Counter-Intelligence Program and

J. Edgar Hoover warned that "an effective coalition of black nationalist groups might be the first step toward a real 'Mau Mau' in America, the beginning of a true black revolution." Malcolm, "our shining black prince," was assassinated a week later.

SNCC

The number of students doubled in the decade; there were more students than farmers. The University had become the focal point of national growth. These youngsters were militants; the militants were students. University at the time didn't cost much. There were, however, fewer of them. Still, students were relatively privileged.

In the spring of 1960, there was the execution in San Quentin of Caryl Chessman by gassing. There was the Sharpeville massacre in South Africa. These shocked the young idealists of the time. Then there was the approval of the birth control pill, which seemed to open the way to massive lovemaking. Ed Sanders wrote, "two roads seemed to split the American vista: fun & revolution."

Revolution or fun were the alternatives in America. The fun corrupted into porn, the revolution into violence. The American vista became an ugly horizon of terror. The jubilee we observe is one for students, not for the New Left, which in any case began in 1956. SNCC and SDS sang their songs, expressed their hopes, plotted their campaigns, danced their dances, took the hand of history saying good-bye to the old steps. These new dances started out as a cup of coffee at a lunch counter. It was fifty years ago. Now fifty years is the jubilee of something. Jubilee used to mean (the pick digs deep) emancipation, debt cancellation, the return of lands, the reclamation of commons, and rest. In bringing it back and taking it forward, we could do worse than these ancient Near Eastern practices.

February 1, 1960: the sit-in at the Woolworth lunch counter in Greensboro, North Carolina, and a few weeks later in April, Ella Baker brought together the students who founded SNCC. Howard Zinn, a young professor, helped out the SNCC students. He wrote of them, "They have no closed vision of the ideal community. They are fed up with what has been; they are open to anything new and are willing to start from scratch." "They are young radicals; the word 'revolution' occurs again and again in their speech. Yet they have no party, no ideology, no creed." They believed in action, and their actions spoke louder than words.

A nineteen-year-old white student wrote, "the University is not much different than a giant marketplace of mediocrity, an extension of a corrupt, warped, illusion-ridden, over-commercialized, superficial society whose basic purpose seems to be turning out students to be good citizens—dead, unconscious automatons in our hysterically consuming society. I want to work in the South as this seems to be the most radical (to the core), crucial, and important place to begin to try and enlarge the freedom of humanity."

SNCC stood for nonviolent direct action, the "beloved community," and antiracism. As students they stayed up all night talking about existentialism, philosophy, theology, French literature. They did it in jail, not the classroom. From its credo composed at Raleigh, NC, 1960: "We affirm the philosophical or religious ideal of nonviolence as the foundation of our purpose, the presupposition of our faith, and the manner of our action. Love is the central motif of nonviolence." They appealed to conscience and the moral nature of human existence. It was philosophy, or spirituality, or a love that enabled them to take a beating and by doing so beat down segregation.

Howard Zinn wrote that the best approach is "boldness in moving into situations where interracial contact will take place, and then patience in letting them develop." Things began to get desperate in the winter of 1960–61 in McComb County, Mississippi, as local forces prevented even federal food from being provisioned to the hungry and starving. Instead caravans of clothing and food from Michigan, some from Ann Arbor, began to arrive. This was a kind of commoning, though no one called it that at the time.

Staughton Lynd remembers a SNCC staff meeting on June 12, 1964. He wrote, "Several staff members said this week: I'm ready to die, but I need a program worth dying for. I think that both for the movement's effectiveness and for its morale there really must be more thinking as to program." A few days later Goodman, Schwerner, and Chaney were assassinated. So voter registration and membership in the Democratic Party became the "program" as a default for want of having done that thinking as to program, and even they were betrayed at the Atlantic City convention that summer, by the Dems, the liberals, and the UAW. The question remains, what is the program to die for?

SDS

In 1901, Upton Sinclair spoke at the founding of the Intercollegiate Socialist Society, which was to become the League for Industrial Democracy. "Since the professors would not educate the students, it was up to the students to educate the professors." Early on Jack London said, "Raise your voices one way or the other; be alive."

In August 1959, SLID (Student League for Industrial Democracy) changed its name to SDS and in the following spring the first SDS convention was held here in Ann Arbor. "Human Rights in the North" was the conference's name.

SNCC vitalized the meeting. The students were black and white, from the north and south. The UAW provided a grant "to look for radical alternatives to the inadequate society."

Dwight MacDonald spoke on "The Relevance of Anarchism." The students asked, "What is happening to us, where are we going, what can we do?"

The preamble to its constitution affirmed that SDS "maintains a vision of a democratic society, where at all levels the people have control of the decisions which affect them and the resources on which they are dependent." At the beginning they were drawing upon and revising classic socialist and anarchist ideas but without taking a stand in the stultifying Cold War ideologies. Al Haber wrote in 1961, "The synthesis continually in our mind is that which unites vision and relevance."

The poet Ed Sanders summarized the "Port Huron Statement" (1962), which, he writes, "cut free of Cold War commie-noia & free of the do-nothing component of the labor movement." It was produced in an interesting way. In the summer of 1961, questionnaires were sent out to the entire membership asking for its views. The answers were then sent to all asking for changes. These became the basis of another submission to the membership and further review. Tom Hayden prepared a draft for the Port Huron conference. There, workshops discussed each issue, and both big issues (bones) and little ones (widgets) were submitted for discussion and vote at a plenary meeting. This then became the basis of a final draft.

"We are the inheritors and the victims of a barren period in the development of human values." "The role of the intellectuals and of the universities (and therefore, I think, SDS) is to enable people to actively enjoy the common life and feel some sense of genuine influence over their personal and collective affairs."

Student comes from Latin, meaning to be eager or zealous, or diligent. SDS members were questioners whose investigations thoughtfully and empirically gathered knowledge in a way similar to that followed by Karl Marx or Richard Wright. And then they attempted to put this knowledge to work.

SDS formed economic research and action projects (ERAP). SDS stood for participatory democracy and anti-anticommunism. SNCC stood for antiracism and the "beloved community." Thus each came close to naming the commons, but both skirted the idea in important ways, one with a nimbus of spirituality and the other with the convolution of a double-negative (anti-anticommunism), which made it difficult to grasp and develop the idea.

After the summer of 1964, the movement began to change under the impact of the looming war in Vietnam and then the nefarious activity of the COINTEL program of the FBI. SNCC began to respond to the call for "Black Power" which issued from the black proletariat of the northern cities and, at the same time, it became increasingly conscious of the international dimension of national liberation movements. Martin Luther King moved to Chicago. SDS began to disintegrate after the Democratic Convention of 1968 when the Blue Meanies of Chicago ran amok.

Black Panthers

Although the symbol itself arose from the voter registration campaigns of the south (Lowndes County), the Black Panther Party, founded in 1966, quickly became an organization of the urban north and west, Chicago, Los Angeles, Detroit, San Diego, Denver, Newark, New York, Boston, Philadelphia, Pittsburgh, Cleveland, Seattle, Washington, DC. The party's Ten-Point Program included employment, housing, health care, justice, peace, and education. It began as a self-defense organization against police brutality and quickly developed other forms of autonomous living, most notably, the free breakfast programs for children, the free medical clinics for the sick and infirm, the door-to-door health services, and the free schooling.

In Chicago, Fred Hampton was effective in bringing about a nonaggression pact among the street gangs by persuading them to desist from crime and by teaching the elements of solidarity in the class struggle. He formed alliances with other organizations. It was he who coined the expression "the rainbow coalition." The Chicago police and the FBI assassinated him in December 1969. He had said, "You can kill the revolutionary but not the revolution."

Now, having sketched the history of May Day and linked it to the jubilee of SNCC and SDS, we arrive at the third task of this sketch, the invitation to President Barack Obama to join the immigrants rights march in Detroit the afternoon of May Day in 2010 after addressing the students at Michigan's Big House. By all means let him come, but let him come as one man, a person among many, but not as president. As such he is too entangled in the toils of the ruling class. Not so long ago, for instance, he directed the largest immigration raid in American history, eight hundred officers of ICE (Immigration and Customs Enforcement) in South Tucson.

Obama and You

Obama's book, *Dreams from My Father: A Story of Race and Inheritance* (1995), is a compelling autobiography, and it remains a commercial success. Notice it is about "dreams." It is a "story." It is about an "inheritance." The biographical approach underestimates historical forces. In searching for his father in Indonesia, Kenya, and a father-like patrimony in Chicago, he underestimates the historical experience of the fathers. Both in Kenya and in Java, they avoided the deaths attendant on the terrorizing enclosure of common lands, but the defeat nevertheless affected them, even while they seemed to prosper in new petroleum-related jobs.

People who grow up with their parents' defeat take that as the norm. Their personality is shaped accordingly and so it has been with Obama. Personalities are not fixed forever. We are a collective subjectivity. The surge of historical change makes it possible in long lifetimes to pass through several. Can we grasp the living spirit of human experience, hold it in our hand? America is full of second acts, and makeovers. We want to see through Obama as if he were a window and not a mirror of our projections. To do this we need to understand the dreams of his father's generation, which had been killed even before he was born. They survived terror, massacre, imprisonment, loss.

Our identity stems not just from our fathers, it is not just our family; our humanity must scale upward beyond genetic lineages. Who are we to become? The big forces—war, globalization, climate change, automobilism, expropriation from land—arise through time and the conflict of classes: between the rulers and the ruled (power), the many and the few (numbers), the haves and the have-nots (possessions), the working class and the capitalist class (twentieth century), the privatizer and the commoner (twenty-first century). Prophetic generalization requires us to adhere to historical specificity.

When the boy, Obama, arrived in Indonesia, his stepfather fetched him. "We stopped at the common, where one of Lolo's men was grazing a few goats." Obama learned how to box, to take a punch, and to deal with beggars, but the commons was being expropriated. Otherwise silence awaited him. What were the dreams, not from his father, but of his father? Obama's stepfather in Indonesia had survived the massacres of 1965–66 by silence. Moreover, he prospered to the extent that he obtained employment in the petroleum industry. By the time he enters the young Obama's life, he has put the past behind him. Yet the present is nothing more than the accumulated past.

Obama's biological father in Kenya also survived and prospered during the struggle for freedom from the imperial government of Great Britain. Frantz Fanon taught us to understand these movements as both freedom movements and movements of bourgeois nationalism. What were the aspirations of Mau Mau? For if bourgeois nationalism expressed the right-wing aspect of the liberation struggle, what was the left-wing aspect? It depended on a relationship to the forest and commoning. They were smashed by British terrorism—concentration camps and hangings.

When Obama came to the continental United States to begin to search for authorities here, how was he going to fit in? Eventually, after several colleges, many chameleon changes, he settled in Chicago, and here too he fell into a time of silence, repression, defeat.

In Indonesia, Africa, and Chicago, Toer, Fanon, and Wright provide us the materials, the clue, to understanding the structural silences. For in all of those writers it is not difficult to discern elements of commoning as a relation to land, to community, and to class. The anchors of doctrine or union or schooling provide no purchase in the storm. It is one where hope is chimerical, unrelated to either political programs or the movements to the commons.

Class consciousness is the knowledge that emancipation is ours. Class struggle is the fight for it, the fight to be a class and then the fight to abolish the class system. It is not economistic; it is historical. It was concrete not abstract. It was expressed in real voices, voices of the past and voices of the present. The skill is in the listening.

The pick pierces the soil or shale. The pick also acts as a lever. Thus, the usefulness of the pick arises from two functions. It penetrates its subject, and it dislodges it. As historians we do the same. It takes an energy from the past to heat and light the present. The lever-and-fulcrum uses distance to increase force. The class of working people can move the world. We need to recognize one another. The bowl of seeds is an artifact of preservation. It permits a future life. So, look at these seeds from our past—the eight-hour day, commoning, nonviolent direct action, one big union, song, *satyagraha*, participatory democracy—and watch them grow. They require sufficient aeration, which we provide by talking and debate; they require plenty of watering, which our considered and righteous action supplies. Then they germinate in many forms: horizontal unionism, solidarity economics, commoning, autonomous living, Social Forums . . . Fellow worker Obama is welcome, but not his executive power. Our power arises from our class, and it is that which we must make. Hence, you and I are urgently needed.

Further Reading

Brownhill, Leigh. *Land, Food, Freedom: Struggles for the Gendered Commons in Kenya*. Trenton, NJ: Africa World Press, 2009.

Geertz, Clifford. *Agricultural Involution: The Process of Ecological Change in Indonesia*. Berkeley: University of California Press, 1963.

Green, James. *Death in the Haymarket: A Story of Chicago, the First Labor Movement and the Bombing That Divided Gilded Age America*. New York: Pantheon Books, 2006.

Grubačić, Andrei, ed. *From Here to There: The Staughton Lynd Reader*. Oakland: PM Press, 2010.

Morton, Thomas. *The New English Canaan*. Amsterdam: J.F. Stam, 1637.

Obama, Barack. *Dreams from My Father: A Story of Race and Inheritance*. New York: Times Books, 1995.

Sale, Kirkpatrick. *SDS*. New York: Random House, 1973.

Sanders, Ed. *America: A History in Verse*, vols. 1–3. Santa Rosa, CA: Black Sparrow Press, 2000, 2004; *America: A History in Verse: The 20th Century*. Woodstock, NY: Blake Route Press, 2008. CD-ROM.

Shiva, Vandana. *Stolen Harvest: The Hijacking of the Global Food Supply*. Boston: South End Press, 2000.

Toer, Pramoedya Ananta. *The Mute's Soliloquy*. Translated by Willem Samuels. New York: Penguin, 1999.

Wright, Richard. *The Color Curtain: A Report on the Bandung Conference.* Cleveland: World Pub. Co., 1956.

Zinn, Howard. *SNCC: The New Abolitionists.* Boston: South End Press, 2002.

NINE

Archiving with MayDay Rooms

(2011)

None are the historian's pleasures that surpass the finding of a new archive unless it's starting one. It was with boyish excitement that I discovered from the man with the cigarette on Phoenix Street behind the mighty Mt. Pleasant postal sorting depot in Clerkenwell, London, that he worked right there in the British Postal Museum & Archive—indeed he was the archivist.

Half a dozen of us had wandered over there from the Marx Memorial Library at 37a Clerkenwell Green where, as part of a process of animating my part of the archive of the *Zerowork* project of the 1970s, I had been talking about the prisoner movement back then. *Zerowork* was a small journal of "working class" revolutionary analysis and theory which attempted to tie in the auto, mining, welfare, and university struggles to the Keynesian and capitalist crisis. To start off I'd said it was a project where the hippy met the tankie (to use the term for the rigid Stalinist who'd send in the tanks at the slightest deviations from the line). But we were "discovering" not the waged, as the force of historical change, but the power of the wageless, or the houseworkers, the peasants, and the prisoners, thanks to the rising of the women and the worldwide people of color.

A new archive is being established in London as part of an exciting enterprise called MayDay Rooms, which will soon be installed at 88 Fleet Street. MayDay Rooms organized a series of meetings "Round About Midnight" in order "to open the boxes." Their idea was to map the tributaries of the Midnight Notes operation of pamphlets, books, and half-pints (as we called our quarto productions). *Zerowork*, the New York Wages for Housework, and the Committee for Academic Freedom in Africa all agreed to deposit their records with MayDay Rooms. Silvia Federici, George Caffentzis, and I gave background presentations on these different tributaries over three days.

For my part, I deposited a run of twenty different issues of *NEPA News: The Voice of the New England Prisoners' Association, 1973–1975*. Prisoners fought for citizen observation, prisoners fought for unions. The Attica Massacre of September 1971 set it off, and the assassination of George Jackson set off Attica. He had been a teenager and robbed a filling station. He had written, "Capitalism is the enemy. It must be destroyed. There is no other recourse. Each individual born in these Amerikan cities should be born with those things that are necessary to survival. Meaningful social roles, education, medical care, food, shelter, and understanding should be guaranteed at birth. They have been part of all civilized human societies—until this one. Why else do men allow other men to govern?"

On one side was "zerowork," and on the other side . . . well, let George Gissing, the Victorian novelist, explain. He wrote in *The Nether World* (1889) about Clerkenwell. There you could see "how men have multiplied toil for toil's sake, have wrought to devise work superfluous, have worn their lives away in imagining new forms of weariness." Historically Clerkenwell was filled with watchmakers and jewelers in tiny workshops where cunning fingers and contriving brains produced those wheels within wheels that William Blake said destroyed the imagination, stunted the mind, and made slavish and dull the human person. "Wealth inestimable is ever flowing through these workshops, and the hands that have been stained with gold-dust, as likely as not, some day extend themselves in petition for a crust." Dens full of hungry children awaited their mother's return with her chance earnings.

In our day, the traces of our radical movements are being thrown into rubbish pits, as state-sponsored "austerity" demands the commodification of every inch of space, and with sinister intent destroys the evidence of our past, its joys, its victories. Clear out the closets, empty the shelves, toss out the old footage, shred the underground press, pulverize the brittle, yellowing documents! Thus neoliberalism organizes the transition from the old to the new; they must silence alternatives. We do not want the voice of George Jackson to be silenced. His words still eloquently describe a desirable program, a necessary program. This is the need that brought about the project of MayDay Rooms run by a remarkable collective of activist scholars, artists, and teachers, and sponsored by the Glass House Trust.

As for Clerkenwell Green it had been a staging area for the peasants who had come to London in 1381 to demand the return of their commons. The London Corresponding Society, the first democratic society, met just east of the Green in Jerusalem Passage. The Clerkenwell mob kept recruiting offices out of the Green. Here Henry Hunt spoke for Parliamentary reform, and William Cobbett opposed the Corn Laws. In 1832 the National Union of the Working Classes met here. In 1842 the prime minister actually "banned meetings on Clerkenwell Green." John Stuart Mill helped make No. 37a a place of meeting of the London Patriotic Club where Eleanor Marx, Peter Kropotkin, and William Morris spoke.

At the Marx Memorial Library we met in a room dedicated to the International Brigades, who had fought against fascism in Spain during its civil war. This was an archive too. Dating from 1737 the building had become a meeting place. The Bolshevik Lenin had studied here in exile, his study actually was above us where the *Iskra* ("the Spark") was edited. Hanging from a wall was the banner designed by Morris of the Hammersmith Socialist Society.

It was here in 1966 that the late Eric Hobsbawm had kindly arranged for me to look at the English translation of Marx's decisive articles on the criminalization of custom, or the "theft of wood," in the Moselle Valley thus enabling him (and us) to analyze the transition from the commons to communism. It was here that I met Johnny Williamson, the "dangerous Scot," who had been a CP organizer in the 1934 Toledo General Strike, so important to my university and so important (along with the general strikes of the San Francisco dockers and the Minneapolis Teamsters) to the passage of the Social Security Act, the Wagner Act, and the Act for Aid to Families to Dependent Children. The New Deal program, or the welfare state, now in ruins.

In 1966 Johnny Williamson pointed to the first translation by Helen MacFarlane of *The Communist Manifesto* hanging on the wall protected in glass casing. "A frightful hobgoblin stalks through Europe. We are haunted by a ghost, the ghost of Communism" is how she rendered the passage more familiarly known to us as "A spectre is haunting Europe—the spectre of Communism." Look into the etymology or the philology of "hobgoblin" and "spectre" and you'll find the difference between revolutionary intellectual abstraction and the gothic of the peasant's lore of the commons. Be that as it may.

We met at Marx House because the MayDay Rooms' Fleet Street venue is under renovation, with a planned completion sometime this spring, for activists, comrades, and citizen archivists who alone can animate it.

Well, if archivery is a pleasure only rarely surpassed in the historian's craft, it just might be superseded by the pleasure of the *flaneur*, the person who strolls the streets, loafing at corners, getting lost, chatting with strangers, pausing for a smoke, casting a glance at the scene. Wandering is a methodology inherent to discovery.

> I wander thro' each charter'd street,
> Near where the charter'd Thames does flow
> And mark in every face I meet
> Marks of weakness, marks of woe.

The poem is "London" by William Blake, published in 1794 in *Song of Experience*. He hears in every voice "mind-forg'd manacles" and then provides three examples. One is how the chimney sweeper's cry "Every blackning Church appalls," which conjoins the themes of the period, child labor, industrial pollution, and fundamentalist bigotry. A second example is how the

> Hapless Soldier's sigh
> Runs in blood won Palace walls

In fact the headline in *The Guardian* newspaper the day I arrived in London declared how Prince Harry had "killed" from his helicopter in Afghanistan. Thus royalty in the twenty-first century teaches young men the meaning of "manhood." The magic of royalty, the mystique of sovereignty, has always depended on murder as sublime. And then Blake's third example is

> How the youthful Harlot's curse
> Blasts the new born Infant's tear
> And blights with plagues the Marriage hearse.

Prostitution and STDs awaited the young women coming to town. Their children uncared for, syphilis abounding, and the structures of social and human reproduction corrupted by the most devastating policies of prison, enclosures, prostitution, factories, slavery, and war. Violence was widespread and universal; violence against women was specific and particular. The era produced Thomas Malthus, the population "explosion," and the devouring of lives in the gaping maw of war. For men, killing. For women, breeding.

So, in wandering the streets with an old Ordnance Survey map of Clerkenwell in hand, I quickly found that Clerkenwell Green was surrounded by sites of prisons, workhouses, dungeons, madhouses, and institutional enclosures. The carceral was the principle that laid out this neck of the woods. The pavement itself seemed marked with weakness, with woe. A Clerkenwell real estate magnate had erected a house for one hundred "fallen women."

Anthony Davies of MayDay Rooms took me to the site of Middlesex House of Detention, where a kindly porter guided us through a parking lot of upscale vehicles (BMW, Volvo, Mercedes) to a lichen- and moss-covered brick wall upon which was attached a plaque commemorating it as the exact place where a gunpowder explosion had breached the walls in an attempt to rescue the Fenians, or Irish freedom fighters, in 1867. Nine were killed and forty injured.

This was a notorious prison built in 1775. In W.J. Pinks's outstanding and unsurpassed *History of Clerkenwell* (1881) he described its prisoners as lamentably ignorant and superstitious, taking "great delight in sitting in a ring and telling their adventures and relating their dreams; they tell stories of spirits." Precisely! It was against these adventures, dreams, stories, and spirits that the system of solitary confinement had been introduced, including another prison called the Middlesex House of Correction erected in 1794.

Edward Marcus Despard, the abolitionist, the United Irishman, and Jacobin revolutionary, suffered under that system at Cold Bath Fields Prison from 1798–1800. The prison was erected in the same year Blake wrote "London," and it was named after the bathers who had believed the waters of the Fleet River here possessed healing properties. Actually, the common people called it "the Steel," short for the Bastille, and in truth it was erected as part of the enclosing repression against the ideas of *liberté*, *égalité*, and *fraternité*, and there was nothing at all rehabilitative or reformative about it whatsoever. Of all the mind-forged manacles it was the key. It closed off those dreams and stories. But even such totalitarianism, the dream of total control and incessant labor, such as Jeremy Bentham proposed that year with his "panopticon," was incomplete because, as we used to say, "the power of the people is stronger than the man's technology."

The Angela Davis of the time, the Michelle Alexander or Ruthie Gilmore of the day, was a woman, a revolutionary, named Catherine Despard. She organized a remission of Edward's unjustifiable incarceration without trial; she lobbied Parliament successfully; she stirred up the press to see the imprisonment as a scandal; she caused some politicians to become active against the cruelties of the place and its governor; she organized the wives of the other political prisoners; I do not know what part she played, if any, in the riotous demonstrations that took place outside the walls in the open fields and common lands to the north of the prison walls. Together and in combination all of these efforts succeeded and he was released. Bentham's totalitarian panopticon was never actually realized thanks to her.

Catherine was an African American to use our terminology; at the time she was described as a Negro or a creole. However, the point is not her ethnicity. The point is the relation between ethnicity and historical experience. She came from that part of the world proletariat that had most experience in the struggle for liberation; I mean the slaves of North America, or their descendants and affines.

Clerkenwell is not only an archipelago of enclosures. Enclosure is never absolute: there are always means of getting under, over, through, or around.

On the north side of Mount Pleasant (named because it had been a noisome trash and ordure mound) is Calthorpe Street, where one of the new police had been killed in an affray of 1831 and the London jury famously found the democrats indicted for the fact not guilty, by reason of "justifiable homicide."

Then a few yards away was Spa Fields. Here a massive and dangerous insurrection, led by Spencean Philanthropists, broke out in the winter of 1816–17 with starving soldiers, sailors, and Clerkenwell workers, which sent such a shudder through the higher echelons of the gentrified classes that even Jane Austen was compelled to notice it with a fright.

The archivist at the Mount Pleasant Museum and Archive explained to me that with the decline of letters and parcels (lost to the internet) the huge post office depot was moving. It had been established, he explained, in 1887 on top of "the Steel," the old Cold Bath Fields Prison. Remains of its cells could still be found underground in the basements of the building. Thus, quite by accident, I had found the location of Despard's incarceration; my feet were treading too on the grounds where Mrs. Despard had remonstrated. Thus did wandering complement the archiving.

On my way back to Marx House I noticed the silhouette of the city of London was no longer dominated by the restful dome of St. Paul's. What was that huge spire-like structure to its east? I asked a nearby stranger having a smoke on the sidewalk. "We call it 'the Shard,'" he explained in Irish brogue. "The bottom storeys are for offices, and the top floors are the condos for the billionaires whose names I cannot pronounce."

"They're now talking of trillionaires," I added irrelevantly.

"Yes, trillions," he agreed, and flicking away the fag end of his roll up, departed saying "what we need is mass insurrection."

I happily made my way back to Marx Memorial House and the wonderful archiving of the MayDay Rooms knowing that our efforts of preservation of that movement George Jackson had defined cannot be obliterated.

Further Reading

Ackroyd, Peter. *London: The Biography*. New York: Nan A. Talese, 2000.

Alexander, Michelle. *The New Jim Crow: Mass Incarceration in the Age of Colorblindness*. New York: The New Press, 2011.

Austen, Jane. *Northanger Abbey*. 1817.

Blake, William. *Songs of Innocence and Experience*. 1789, 1794.

Davis, Angela Y. *Are Prisons Obsolete?* New York: Seven Stories Press, 2003.

Gilmore, Ruth Wilson. *The Golden Gulag: Prisons, Surplus, Crisis, and Opposition in Globalizing California*. Berkeley: University of California Press, 2007.

Gissing, George. *The Nether World*. 1889.

Jackson, George. *Soledad Brother*. New York: Bantam Books, 1970.

Marx, Karl. *The Communist Manifesto*. 1848.

TEN

Ypsilanti Vampire May Day

(2012)

Dedicated to the students, young and old, of southeastern Michigan and northwestern Ohio

Dracula

On May Day sometime in the 1890s, an ordinary Englishman boarded a train in Munich.[1] His destination was a castle in Transylvania, a country wedged between the Danubian provinces of Moldavia and Wallachia. It was a dark and stormy night when he arrived, and the wind was howling hard.

"Do you not know that tonight, when the clock strikes midnight, all the evil things of the world will have full sway?" asked the landlady of a nearby hotel, and she implored him to reverse his course. Other commoners then warned him it was a witch's Sabbath. Heedless, he persisted to the castle where pure terror awaited him in the personage of a blood-sucking monster. Count Dracula was at once as smooth, polite, and persuasive as President Obama, and as terrifying, shape-shifting, and diabolical as George W. Bush. He was undead—a zombie, or a werewolf—and lived only as long as he was able to suck human blood.

---

1 Thanks to Kate Hutchens of the University of Michigan Library's Labadie Collection; to the Ypsilanti Historical Society; to Constantine George Caffentzis; to Kate Khatib of AK Press; to Professor Ronald Grigor Suny; to Anna of Thessaloniki; to Lia Yoka of Thessaloniki; to Jeffery Pollock and Eric Albjerg of the University of Toledo; and to Michaela Brennan and Riley Linebaugh.

As for the crisis of our own lives, in 2009 Matt Taibbi assigned blame to the banks, calling Goldman Sachs "a great vampire squid wrapped around the face of humanity, relentlessly jamming its blood funnel into anything that smells like money."[2] Reverend Edward Pinkney of Benton Harbor, Michigan, referring to the emergency manager which was wrapped around the face of his city, said "he's for the corporations that suck the life out of people." Banks, insurance companies, and corporations belong to the total circuit of capitalism whence the sucking originates. When Alan Haber, the first president of Students for a Democratic Society (SDS), spoke last winter at the Crazy Wisdom Book Shop and Tea Room in Ann Arbor about his experiences at Occupy Boston and Occupy Wall Street, he concluded his remarks by reminding everybody that "Capital is dead labor, which vampire-like, lives only by sucking living labor, and lives the more, the more labor it sucks."

As May Day 2012 approaches Ypsilanti, by all means let us tell stories of flowers and fertility rituals and of the ancient festivals on the commons; and let us, for sure, commemorate the great struggle for the eight-hour workday that reached a climax in Chicago at the Haymarket in May 1886, and gave birth to the holiday of workers around the planet, east and west, north and south. As the prospect of the appointment of an emergency manager looms over Ypsilanti—with powers to abrogate union contracts, close schools, sell public assets, expropriate municipal lands, and whose very word is law—we must also greet the day with the realistic gloom that comes from an uncertainty about health, roof, studies, and livelihood. The tooth is at our throat!

---

2   Matt Taibbi, "The Great American Bubble Machine," *Rolling Stone*, July 9, 2009, http://www.rollingstone.com/politics/news/the-great-american-bubble-machine-20100405.

Our green parks are turned into toxic brownfields and our common lands have been laid waste as collateral for unspecified "development." Our eight-hour workday is lengthened by multiple part-time jobs, or by the time-consuming caretaking of elders without pensions or children without day care. Our lives now are in the grip of mysterious forces called securitization or financialization, to which we submit in dumbfounded helplessness, though the blush on our faces reminds us that these forces are but the bloodsuckers of old. Voltaire wrote that "stock jobbers, brokers, and men of business sucked the blood of the people in broad daylight . . . these true suckers live not in cemeteries but in very agreeable palaces."[3]

We face a crisis of production, yes, but also a crisis of reproduction. Production pertains to factories, sweatshops, mines, and fields; it is the realm of commerce, technology, and commodities. Reproduction pertains to kitchens, families, schools, neighborhoods; it is the realm of society, service, and a very special "commodity"—actually no commodity at all, rather: human beings. Reproduction takes place over various cycles of duration. It may mean the daily preparation for the next day or week—the shopping, the cooking, the cleaning, etc. Or it may mean the preparation of the next generation, beginning with its creation and extending from diaper changing to graduate school. Michaela Brennan, a public health nurse at the Packard Community Clinic outside Ypsilanti, sighed in near despair: "So many people need looking after!"

Reverend Pinkney and Greece circa 2012

Benton Harbor is on the other side of the state, but its tale is Ypsilanti's too. Reverend Pinkney opposed the expropriation

---

3   *Philosophical Dictionary* (1764).

of the parklands which had been deeded to the city a hundred years ago, to belong to it "forever." Such places are common lands. Whirlpool Corporation wanted the land and so did the developers who had in mind a golf course for executives and the Chicago summer people. The people's park had to go, and so did the people. When they squawked, an emergency manager was forced on the town. Its commons were then privatized by the 1 percent.

One aim of this book is to oppose emergency managers—in the name of democracy!—and, in the name of the commons, to oppose the capitalist system behind them. We are being hoodwinked.

In 2007 Reverend Pinkney quoted scriptures to a judge:

> Cursed shalt thou be in the city, and cursed shalt thou be in the field. Cursed shall be thy basket and thy store. Cursed shall be the fruit of thy body, and the fruit of thy land, the increase of thy kine, and the flocks of thy sheep. . . . The Lord shall smite thee with a consumption, and with a fever, and with an inflammation, and with an extreme burning, and with the sword, and with blasting, and with mildew; and they shall pursue thee until thou perish.[4]

The judge found these lines threatening and ordered Edward Pinkney to prison for three to ten years. Pinkney kept up the fight inside jail, where despite the mutual resentment of blacks, whites, and browns, he coordinated with each group and collectively they won better food for themselves.

An emergency manager is a dictator. In ancient Rome, Sulla was one of the patricians who opposed the *populares*, who were still in mourning for the death of the fraternal people's tribunes of Caius and Tiberius Gracchus, whose

---

4   Deuteronomy 28:14–22.

Agrarian Law redistributed the land of the patricians and preserved the common lands of the people, or the *ager publicus*. Sulla ravaged Athens until its streets ran with blood; in Rome he slaughtered five thousand prisoners. Under an emergency, he had himself declared "dictator" and murdered his friends. His word was law, and law was death. The Roman people were offered bread and circuses; we are offered McDonald's and golf. In Benton Harbor the *ager publicus* has been privatized; it now has no people and eighteen holes.

This phenomenon is worldwide. Take Greece, for instance. From Thessaloniki a woman named Anna writes me, "I don't know if you are aware that since last fall, instead of having an elected government, the IMF [International Monetary Fund] and the European Bank have appointed an emergency government to manage the crisis." The manager used to work for Goldman Sachs. He puts the funnel in to draw some blood.

In December of 2008, in an autonomous neighborhood in downtown Athens, a fifteen-year-old high school student named Alexis Grigoropoulos was deliberately shot to death by a policeman. Lia Yoka, another colleague in Greece, writes me that the people of Nafplion—Ypsilanti's sister-city in that country—protested by occupying the Town Council and the Theatre Department of the University of Peloponnese. A generation of young Greek people roused themselves from a decade's torpor and sprung into outrage: high school and university students, immigrants, the unemployed, precarious workers, and others occupied the streets in riotous protest, and turned them into an urban commons. This occurred amid the economic "shock therapy" that has accompanied the response to the Greek debt. A state of exception was declared.

The minimum wage in Greece has been sliced by 25 percent, making it the lowest in Europe. Allowances, benefits, pensions have been destroyed. Youth unemployment is at 51 percent. What was once a welfare state providing relief "from the cradle to the grave" has become a penal state that incarcerates some immigrants in special detention units and criminalizes others, including those who wear hoodies! Six out of ten Greek households are in arrears with their mortgage payments; seven out of ten are in arrears with consumer loans; one out of two are in arrears with credit card payments. This is a crisis of reproduction, and women are the hardest hit.

Fiscal terrorism operates emotionally as well as economically. Crisis is experienced as a multitude of personal failures; collective guilt and self-blame become commonplace, and neither trade unionism nor politicians have been able to respond successfully. One-day general strikes, sectional strikes by subway workers, bus drivers, secondary school teachers, hospital doctors, bank employees, and truck drivers have also been unable to halt the bulldozing of the Greek working class. Suicides have increased. The most effective antidepressant is collective action, yet this is criminalized.

The situation does indeed resemble Count Dracula's castle: the barred windows of banks; the impregnable battlements of securitization; the bolted doors of financialization; the endless corridors of credit default swaps; the twisting stairways of lost mortgages; the heavy portcullis of fiscalism. Every view is hemmed in by enclosure, and each citizen is watched over by the omniscient Evil Eye of surveillance cameras. Even the Greek minister of labor has declared "there will be blood."[5] We yearn to escape.

---

5   I am especially grateful to two articles by "Children of the Gallery," a Greek collective: "The Rebellious Passage of a Proletarian Minority through a Brief Period of Time" and "Burdened with Debt: 'Debt Crisis' and Class Struggles in Greece," in *Revolt and Crisis in Greece:*

Here, then, as if from a nineteenth-century poet, is an Ypsilanti vampire story; only, this is not just a story. It is real, instructive, and documented history and may also be a shadow from the future cast back onto the past. It may—it should—curdle your blood, quicken your heart, and rouse you to fury. We have been bamboozled.

Debamboozling

Howard Zinn's *A People's History of the United States* was first published in 1980. Even if you possess only a single shelf for books and spices, this should be on it, right next to the salt! What is radical history? Zinn quotes sociologist E. Franklin Frazier, as he speaks to black college students in Atlanta: "All your life, white folks have bamboozled you, preachers have bamboozled you, teachers have bamboozled you; I am here to debamboozle you."[6]

The B-24 was built at Willow Run in the township of Ypsilanti. As a young bombardier, Howard Zinn did not fly "The Liberator," as the B-24 was called, but instead in a B-17, a "Flying Fortress." Zinn remembers that "the crews who flew those planes [B-24s] died in great numbers. We who flew the more graceful-looking B-17s sardonically called those other planes B dash 2 crash 4." The B-24 had a longer range and could carry a heavier payload, but it tended to catch fire.[7] It was "the worst piece of metal aircraft construction I have ever seen," according to Charles Lindbergh.

Between a Present Yet to Pass and a Future Still to Come, eds. Antonis Vradis and Dimitris Dalakoglou (Oakland and London: AK Press and Occupied London, 2011), 115–31, 245–78. I am also grateful for a message from Anna in Thessaloniki.

6   Howard Zinn, *The Politics of History* (Boston: Beacon Press, 1970), 45.

7   Howard Zinn, "The Greatest Generation?" *The Progressive* 65 (October 2001): 12–13. See also his *Failure to Quit: Reflections of an Optimistic Historian* (Monroe, ME: Common Courage Press, 1993), and *You Can't Be Neutral on a Moving Train: A Personal History of Our Times* (Boston: Beacon Press, 1993).

Of World War II, Zinn wrote, "I thought it was a just cause. Therefore you drop bombs." He was the first to drop napalm, which he regretted for the rest of his life, and lived to remember a pilot who perished and who had told him, "You know, this is not a war against fascism. It's a war for empire. England, the United States, the Soviet Union—they are all corrupt states, not morally concerned about Hitlerism, just wanting to run the world themselves. It's an imperialist war." This unnamed casualty debamboozled Howard Zinn, who became one of the most influential peaceniks of the second half of the twentieth century. Like Zinn, Albert Parsons changed his mind. In the Civil War, he had ridden cavalry on behalf of Confederate slave masters. Parsons and Zinn excelled at what they did, but after bitter experience each came to reject as false the virtues of valor and bravery when in service of war or slavery, but as true when in the service of peace and the working class. That is why, comrades, we must *never give up* on those who disagree with us.

At the base of the Ypsilanti water tower there is a marble bust of a Greek who looks grand despite having weathered eighty-four years since its creation. Demetrios Ypsilantis stares into the Michigan skies, with a splendid high collar to hold up his chin, dashing military braids to enlarge his chest, a gallant sash, and brush-like epaulettes that broaden his shoulders.

Demetrios and his brother Alexander, an *aide-de-camp* to Alexander I, Czar of Russia, had been officers in the military of the Russian Empire until the spring of 1821 when Alexander Ypsilantis, along with a small contingent, invaded Moldavia from the east; Demetrios entered Wallachia from the west. They thus fought the first battles of the decade-long war of Greek independence from the Ottoman Empire. It is an accident of history that the Greek War of Independence commenced in the Danubian provinces of Moldavia and

Wallachia, the very region and setting of *Dracula*. And there is still more to it: in these same provinces we discover a key genesis of the transition from expropriation to exploitation which characterizes capitalist modernity and the crisis we currently suffer. We confront three losses: the loss of blood, the loss of names, and the loss of commons. Only as a result of such a confrontation may we regard May Day and the beauty it promises. A Green beauty and a Red promise.

1. The Loss of Blood

The Battle of Waterloo put an end to Napoleon. Across Europe the jaws of a devouring darkness clamped upon the light of freedom. The wars against the French Revolution were finally over. Crippled soldiers and emaciated sailors returned home to haunt and to starve in city slums. The enclosed peasantry of England cried "bread or blood." The gallows executed followers of Ned Ludd. The mechanization of production had begun. Anyone who dared even peep in demurral was imprisoned. Ireland was smashed; starvation prevailed. In America, slaveholders and Indian-killers ruled supreme.

Giant landlords owned England, the country that Percy Shelley, Mary Shelley, and Lord Byron fled. In an immense carriage that carried his library, dining service, and *lit de repos*, Byron roamed across Europe to Switzerland. One famous evening of idleness and boredom, on the shores of Lake Geneva, these friends amused themselves by telling ghost stories. Mary Shelley told her *Frankenstein* tale, and Byron told a story which his physician, Dr. John Polidori, wrote down and published in 1819. It was a story titled *The Vampyre*.

The stories were cathartic allegories of the historical forces engulfing Lord Byron and the Shelleys: slavery, or proletarianization, and mechanization, or technological innovation. These were the means by which the ruling class squeezed every drop of surplus labor from the people. Slavery forces more people to work harder. Migrations, the Middle Passage, child labor, natalism for women, expropriation from land and subsistence: people are forced to enter factories or plantations. And what is it, this "factory," if not a former West African slave-trading post and subsequently a housing for coal-fired steam engines? Machines merely made things more cheaply, using less labor per unit, and made more units in gross profusion. Human endeavor amounts no longer in cornucupia but in waste dumps.

How did this exploitation work? Alienation turned human beings into zombies, the undead. Monstrous forces sucked the life from women and men: either they produced absolute surplus value, or else they produced relative surplus value. The former lengthened the entire working day, while the latter shortened only that part of it which produced necessary value. But what is this value, and how is it extracted? *Frankenstein* was the prototypical tale of the hidden forces of technology and of the Faustian pride of creation. The technocrat combines the new, scarcely understood energy of electricity and applies it to body parts that have been collected by body snatchers, and in so doing he creates a new kind of creature. The tale's subtitle compares him to Prometheus, the Greek demigod who stole fire from the gods and used it to create humankind.

Frankenstein was published in 1818. A year later John Polidori published his prose version of Byron's ghost story, *The Vampyre*. Polidori drew on ancient peasant folklore and started a craze that reached its apogee with *Dracula*. The protagonist of *The Vampyre* is a philhellene—a lover of Greece and Greek culture—amusing himself in Greece by traipsing over ancient ruins and temples, but who is soon distracted by a beautiful and innocent country girl. He is smitten. In her childhood, her nurse had entertained her with a vampire story whose veracity is confirmed by the old men of the village. The vampire attacks in the woods. "Upon her neck and breast was blood, and upon her throat were the marks of teeth having opened the vein: to this the men pointed, crying, simultaneously struck with horror, 'a Vampyre, a Vampyre!'"

The socioeconomic context of the story is provided by the expropriations of the era. Such superstition "constitutes a sort of religion applicable to the common household necessities of daily life," writes a scholar of that time.[8] Inasmuch as it had functioned to protect the household, the story belongs to the realm of reproduction. And nearly everyone is familiar with this story: what had once been the folklore of an exploited peasantry is now a universal truth for the 99 percent, and as such has become the fable of the world's proletariat. Yet in its first, literary iteration, the bloodsucker became an aristocrat who bides his time with gambling, rape, and the biting of the neck that transforms life into living death. The story's setting is a forest in Greece, and a year later the real forests of the Balkans and Greece will erupt in revolution. Demetrios and Alexander Ypsilantis are at the center of these conflicts.

We must keep these two stories in mind because one is a fable of technology and the intensification of labor, and the other is a fable of slavery and the extension of exploitation.

Philhellenes

By the beginning of the nineteenth century, philhellenism had become a distinct ideology, one with powerful and lasting effects in Europe and America. It arose at the peak of the Atlantic slave trade, and one of its principal effects was the disparagement of Africa. The Nile River Valley, the great pyramids, and Egypt itself were no longer considered the

---

8   Emily Gerard, "Transylvanian Superstitions," *The Nineteenth Century: A Monthly Review* 13 (July–December 1885), 131.

birthplace of civilization. Christian bigotry, the growth of the doctrine of white supremacy, the teleological doctrine of progress, and romantic Hellenism each contributed to philhellenism, which in turn would help justify the expansion of the cotton regime and its death camps, called plantations.[9]

The German concept of *Altertumswissenschaft*, or the science of antiquity, came to dominate research and school curricula. The "Classics"—the Greek and Latin languages—became the foundation of the curriculum at the same time that Greek-letter fraternities originated as chauvinist and anti-intellectual organizations. Sports also originated in the philhellene craze: the 26 miles, 285 yards of the marathon is a distance that commemorates the run of Phidippides, who carried to Athens the news of a Greek victory over the Persians at Marathon, in 490 BCE.

> The mountains look on Marathon—
> And Marathon looks on the sea;
> And musing there an hour alone,
> I dream'd that Greece might still be free.

So Lord Byron mused (*Don Juan*, Canto III, st. 86). After 1821 the love of freedom revived, and the Greek War of Independence commenced, in the wake of a protracted reaction against the French Revolution.[10] Shelley's *Hellas* was composed in 1821 and published the following year: "We are all Greeks. Our laws, our literature, our religion, our arts all have their roots in Greece." Philhellenism begins to turn into hellenomania. "This is the age of the war of the oppressed against oppressors, and every one of those ringleaders of the privileged

9   Martin Bernal, *Black Athena: The Afroasiatic Roots of Classical Civilization*, Vol. 1, *The Fabrication of Ancient Greece, 1785–1985* (New Brunswick, NJ: Rutgers University Press, 1987).
10   William St. Clair, *That Greece Might Still Be Free: The Philhellenes in the War of Independence* (London: Oxford University Press, 1972).

gangs of murderers and swindlers, called Sovereigns, look to each other for aid against the common enemy, and suspend their mutual jealousies in the presence of a mightier fear." True enough.

The philhellenic movement grew in Germany, Russia, and England.[11] All told, a thousand volunteers went to fight in Greece. They were mostly German, French, and Italian, but included in their ranks ninety-nine British and sixteen Americans. Byron (*Don Juan*, Canto VII, st. 18) took a jaundiced view of some.

> Then there were foreigners of much renown,
> Of various nations, and all volunteers;
> Not fighting for their country or its crown,
> But wishing to be one day brigadiers;
> Also to have the sacking of a town,
> A pleasant thing to young men at their years.

Byron himself died in 1824 in Missolonghi, fighting for Greece. In 1824, Samuel Gridley Howe, a Harvard medical student, established a free hospital. Relief committees formed across the United States. In 1826, the Independence movement's greatest enemy was neither the Turks nor the Arabs, but starvation. In 1827, eight shiploads of supplies sailed to Nafplion, Ypsilanti's present-day sister city. Villages had been ruined and tens of thousands massacred. Starving families fled to the mountains and lived on herbs, grass, and worms. The governor of Massachusetts took a Greek orphan into his household.

2. The Loss of Names

The town of Ypsilanti has had other, earlier names. Rev. Mr. Harvey C. Colburn's *The Story of Ypsilanti* (1923) is a history

---

11   L.S. Stavrianos, *The Balkans, 1815–1914* (New York: Holt, Rinehart and Winston, 1963).

of white property-owners *for* white property-owners and therefore relies on an ample paper trail. Frenchman Gabriel Godfroy and his partners claimed large tracts of land by 1811. "The various treaties with the Indians made by Governor St. Clair and the extinguishment of their land claims resulted in their retirement westward." Extinguishment! Land claims! Retirement! This is pure bamboozlement. Robbery, rather.

In 1790 the Potawatomis lived four days upstream from Detroit, in a place known as Sanscrainte's Village among the *coureurs de bois*, the trappers and traders who scorned regulation and married Indian women.[12] Although the land was common, "the women did all the work" of growing peas, corn, beans, and wheat. Jean Baptiste Romain dit Sanscrainte was a *métis*; that is, part Indian and part not. He was a trader and an interpreter in the network of Sauk Trail pelt trappers and traders, and sold, for instance, 73 kegs of whiskey and 170 kegs of tobacco to Anthony Wayne, a commander of the United States Army. In 1795 Sanscrainte signed the Treaty of Greenville, in which Ohio and Michigan lands were ceded by Native Americans.

In September of 1819, Lewis Cass "signed a treaty at Saginaw by which the future Washtenaw County passed forever out of Indian possession." The Potawatomis along the Huron River neglected to harvest their corn and left it standing in their rush to go to Greenville to hear the Shawnee Prophet, who preached sobriety, restraint from wife-beating, and disassociation from the Long Knives (white men). In 1813 the Shawnee Prophet's followers made new villages on the lower Huron River, and a force of Potawatomis established

---

12 Jim Woodruff, *Across Lower Michigan by Canoe 1790* (typescript, Bentley Historical Library, 2004). This is an account of a modern canoe trip following the route taken in 1790 by Hugh Heward as described in his journal. See also Karl Williams, "Gabriel Godfoy Wasn't the First," *Ypsilanti Gleanings* (April 9, 2009).

themselves twenty miles further upstream. Tecumseh's confederacy of Kickapoos, Winnebagos, Sacs, Shawnees, Wyandots, Miamis, Munsee Delawares, Potawatomis, Ojibwas, Ottawas, Senecas, and Creeks retreated to Canada with twelve hundred warriors and their families in canoes. Several hundred Potawatomis refused to budge and remained in their villages on the Huron, under the leadership of Main Poc, a ferocious warrior, bullying drunk, and former foe of the Long Knives.

If this constituted the remnant that was to survive wars and settle in what eventually became Ypsilanti, its recent experience was one of defeat, retreat, and division.[13] The skin must be cut before blood flows. The Founding Fathers made the incision, and the Robber Barons drew the blood.

In 1823 the Woodruff brothers arrived. Sleep was fitful, as they were unfamiliar with the howling of wolves. Indians had prepared the fields for corn, and the European settlers took them over. The indigenous commons was thus expropriated. Some "families bought no farms but squatted on bits of unoccupied land, threw up shacks and proceeded to gain a livelihood in haphazard and dubious manners."[14] This was Woodruff's Grove.

In the spring of 1825: "Land was cleared and fenced, dooryards inclosed and crops planted . . . and the wild life of the forest began to disappear." Augustus Brevoort Woodward—a disciple of President Jefferson, a defender of slave masters, and an expropriator of the Detroit commons—bought the land (612 acres!) and platted the village, naming it Ypsilanti. He had studied Greek at Columbia University, and he published using the pseudonym Epaminondus, a mighty commander in ancient Greece. Woodward was involved in a

13   John Sugden, *Tecumseh* (New York: Henry Holt, 1993), 148, 362.
14   Harvey C. Colburn, *The Story of Ypsilanti* (Ypsilanti Committee on History, 1923), 35, 37, 40.

lucrative Detroit currency and banking swindle. He was also a founder of the University of Michigan, which, possessed as he was by a very strong case of hellenomania, he termed a *catholepistemiad* with thirteen *didaxia*, or professors.[15] He contemplated naming the upper peninsula "Transylvania."

With ax, cart, and plough, "every stroke of his hand made him a capitalist, every uplifting of himself in the new community made of his children ladies and gentlemen." What did this mean? The land is turned into the foundational means of social reproduction; it becomes constant capital, or merely "dead labor" (the Potawatomi land clearings are forgotten) to be revived by "living labor" in the vampiric manner. Within a decade, after the fright of the 1832 Black Hawk War had passed, the first churches, tax assessments, railroad, and banks were established in Ypsi. In that same decade, Wallachia and Moldavia became connected to the Black Sea grain trade. The Danubian provinces thus become the principle supplier of Constantinople, whose bakers now depend on those *boyards* who had expropriated not just the woodlands but the peasant's rights to such commonages.

Michigan toponymy is stratified, with names derived from its past inhabitants. Sanscrainte (*métis*), Godfroy (French), Woodruff (English), Ypsilanti (American). This is the loss of names. Doubtless the name will change again, but exactly when it will change or what its new name will be will depend upon the nature of those who occupy it.

Shall we hasten that day?

Phanariots
The Ypsilantis family were Phanariots, or Greeks who ruled Moldavia and Wallachia on behalf of the Ottoman

---

15   Frank B. Woodford, *Mr. Jefferson's Disciple: A Life of Justice Woodward* (East Lansing: Michigan State College, 1953).

Empire as princes or hospodars, invested by the Grand Vizer of Constantinople as "God's Annointed."[16] Phanariots were named after a lighthouse in the Phanar district of Constantinople. (Is the Ypsilanti city water tower inspired by this lighthouse?) Although they also belonged to the Filiki Eteria, a "society of friends" (modeled on the Italian Carbonari and on Freemasonry) that conspired to lead the Greek War of Independence, the Phanariots were not liked at home. Indeed, an English historian of the region writes, "It is impossible to conceive a more disheartening task than that of recording in detail the history of these hundred years in Wallachia and Moldavia."[17] So many names, so many kings, so much oppression.

Alexander Ypsilantis, Demetrios Ypsilantis's grandfather, had "reformed" the tax code of the Danubian provinces, making it so rigorous "that a peasant would sometimes kill his cattle to escape the . . . cow tax, or even destroy his house to avoid the . . . chimney tax." Young Alexander, brother of Demetrios, encouraged his troops to acts of terror, and it is therefore not surprising that to the peasants he was identified with rapacity and extortion, while to the boyards, or landlords, as an intruder. The common people had a proverb against Phanariot families: "the winter of Hângerli, the earthquake of Ypsilanti, the famine of Moruzi, the pestilence of Caragea." Although Alexander Ypsilantis ignited the war, his ill-disciplined, excessive force did not last long, and others, including the philhellenes, picked up the torch. Alexander himself was confined to a fortress in Munkács, Transylvania!

---

16   Wilkinson, *An Account*, 155–66.
17   R.W. Seton-Watson, *A History of the Roumanians from Roman Times to the Completion of Unity* (Cambridge: Cambridge University Press, 1934), 127.

3. The Loss of Commons

The Greek War of Independence (1820–32) bore certain similarities to the American War of Independence (1775–83): a brilliant outpouring of rhetoric in opposition to empire, and financing from abroad. These wars also resembled each other in an oblique way: they were both land grabs. This is one of the reasons we call them "bourgeois revolutions."

Demetrios Ypsilantis was appointed commander by the Society of Friends. He and his brother were given to making grandiloquent, ceremonious proclamations, and one such proclamation inaugurated the Greek War of Independence. In 1832, following two civil wars, multiple invasions, countless massacres, widespread famine, epidemic pestilence, international diplomacy, and huge bank loans, the war drew to a close.

The common patrimony of a Greek village before the War of Independence was called the *hotar*. "The bulk of the hotar consisted of meadows, grazing, and woodland, and these were used jointly by the whole village." This was the commons. Economically speaking, the commons was a subsistence regime anterior to capitalism. Its disappearance could be sudden or it could occur bit by bit, as was the case in Wallachia and Moldavia. A boyard petition of February 28, 1803, shows that before they could take any surplus from the "boundary," they first had to ask permission from the villagers. The essential customs of the people were traditional and unwritten. "Of these customs evidently none concerned the people so much as their right to the land, a right which remained unaffected by the historical events that were taking place."[18] But a vampire haunted the village borders, which were the location of communal lands.

---

18   David Mitrany, *The Land & the Peasant in Rumania* (London: Oxford University Press, 1930), 7, 9, 17, 19.

In the middle of the eighteenth century some ancient rights (e.g., timber for building and fuel) were granted in exchange for eight to twelve days of labor servitude. But what was a day? It was not measured in the peasant's actual labor time, but fixed "the quantity of labour which, according to its nature, each peasant must perform in one day. This *nart* was twice or thrice as heavy as that which a normal man could do in a normal day."

"The peasants also lost the valuable right to wood for fuel and building which they had enjoyed throughout the worst Turkish times." The first attempt to restrict the peasants' access to timber was in 1792. A British consular report of 1812 recommends a sweeping commercial program—the export of forest timber, and the reduction of fast and feast days to 240![19] In 1820 the British consul observed: "There does not perhaps exist a people laboring under a greater degree of oppression from the effect of despotic power and more heavily burdened with impositions and taxes than the peasants of Wallachia and Moldavia."

The Treaty of Adrianople of 1829 put Russia in charge of Wallachia and Moldavia. Kiselev, a *philosophe* in the school of Voltaire and Diderot, became governor. He was a reformer and passed something like a constitution, the *Réglement Organique*. Boyards sought to restrict peasant cultivation of all lands, with concessions dependent on an extension of days of labor and servitude. The free use of wood from the commons was abolished, and forced service increased to fifty-six days a year. Rents tripled and wheat prices skyrocketed. Karl Marx was upset.

It was Marx, in fact, who said, "Capital is dead labor, which vampire-like, lives only by sucking living labor, and lives the more, the more labor it sucks." You'll find these

---

19   Seton-Watson, *A History of the Roumanians*, 7, 9, 19, 141.

words in "The Working Day," which is the tenth chapter in volume one of *Das Capital*, and is certainly the most powerful description of nineteenth-century capitalism.[20] Part of its power derives from the authenticity of its vampire reference. In part four of this chapter, Marx refers to capitalism's "vampire thirst of the living blood of labor," and in part five he refers to its "blind unrestrainable passion, its werewolf hunger for surplus labor." In the following part he mentions stock-exchange wolves, and concludes the chapter by referring once more to the vampire.[21] Marx drew for this chapter not only upon his massive reading and upon the tireless research of his daughter, but he was also drawing upon the "superstitions of the household" which, as a male Victorian scholar, he would not usually credit.

If not a black man, Karl Marx was certainly dark in complexion, his ancestors having come from Portugal and, before that, from North Africa. His children affectionately called him "the Moor." The Moor defended the people's access to the forest and its resources. What happened in the Balkans would soon happen to the people's estovers in the Moselle River Valley where the Moor grew up. (Estovers is the English name describing wood that a commoner may take; it derives from the French *estover*, or "that which is necessary.") "The community of several thousand souls to which I belong," wrote Marx, "is the owner of most beautiful wooded areas." Statutes and executive orders dating to 1816 distinguish naturally distributed firewood and material for

---

20 I once encountered evidence that German railway workers in St. Louis, Missouri, were the first to translate this tremendous chapter into English, but I've since been unable to track it down.

21 Mark Neocleous, "The Political Economy of the Dead: Marx's Vampires," *History of Political Thought* 24, no. 4 (Winter 2003): 668–84. I also recommend Amedeo Policante, "Vampires of Capigal: Gothic Reflections between Horror and Hope," Cultural Logic, 2010, http:// clogic.eserver.org/2010/Policante.pdf.

making household articles from building timber, if it is not used for communal building or to assist individual members of the community in cases of damage by fire, etc. It was the criminalization of such customs which led Marx to develop his materialist methodology. Nameless timber companies dealing to international markets bought up the forests of the Moselle where Marx's parents had a share in a vine or two. The forests of central and eastern Europe were rapidly being consumed by buyers in western Europe. Marx was as powerless to stop the loss of humble subsistence customs as Warren Kidder was to stop the expropriation of his family farm at Willow Run years later. Because of the distress caused by the lack of firewood in the Moselle and its environs, Marx made plans to write a new article: "The Vampires of the Moselle Region."[22] Look closely and you will find puncture wounds on Marx's neck too.

The temporal coincidence between the Greek War of Independence and the expropriation of the customary rights of peasant commoners, both of which occurred in the 1820s and reached their climaxes in 1832, can be understood in several ways. From the viewpoint of traditional political economy, each was an example of a straightforward transition from "primitive communism" to "capitalist agriculture." From the standpoint of the bourgeoisie, Greece's independence meant liberation from the Ottoman Empire and rebirth as an independent nation-state. From the standpoint of neo-liberalism, it illustrated the conformity between political independence and market relations. For those on the ground, however, it was an emergency: forest, pasturage, and field commons were lost to a regime of increased work, more working days, and more surplus labor. Though it could genuinely appear either as a Greek national liberation struggle

22 *Rheinische Zeitung*, January 15, 1843.

or a transition to capitalism—economic development and modernization—to commoners it was bloodsucking. The destruction of the arboreal canopy in Michigan and in central and eastern Europe occurred at the same time. With the disappearance of Michigan woods "all [was] changed," wrote George Perkins Marsh a few years later. "The face of the earth is no longer a sponge but a dust heap."

Walker's *Appeal* (1829) and the Monstrosity of Race

David Walker, a black Bostonian used-clothes dealer, wrote an *Appeal to the Coloured Citizens of the World* in 1829. In it he challenged the hypocrisy of American support for the Greek independence struggle:

> But oh Americans! Americans! I warn you in the name of the Lord (whether you will hear it or forbear) to repent and reform, or you are ruined ! ! ! Do you think that our blood is hidden from the Lord because you can hide it from the rest of the world, by sending out missionaries and by your charitable deeds to the Greeks, Irish, &c.? Will he not publish your secret crimes on the house top?

On May Day we celebrate the workers of the world: blue collar, white collar, pink collar, in hoodies or prison green, this day belongs to the *entire* working class. It's not the color of her skin but the clothes that maketh the woman. It is a day of *human* agency. Yet the fact remains that in America, built as it is on African slavery, the human beings who led the original workers' struggle were African American. Walker demolished Thomas Jefferson's lame notions of white supremacy, and he did so with stand-up language.

David Walker was born to a slave father and a free mother in North Carolina in 1785. He belonged to the African Methodist Episcopal Church in Charleston, South Carolina, and was to take part in the Denmark Vesey conspiracy, a slave revolt planned for 1822. Slave masters put thousands of dollars on his head. He studied Sparta and the equality of conditions under Lycurgus. The arts and sciences originated in Egypt and then migrated to Greece, according to Walker. People of color "are the most wretched, degraded and abject set of beings that ever lived since the world began."[23] "But I tell you Americans! That unless you speedily alter your course, *you* and your *Country are gone ! ! ! ! !*" He also compares whites to vampires: "The whites have always been an unjust, jealous, unmerciful, avaricious and bloodthirsty set of beings, always seeking after power and authority." He helps us understand that the system of racism is a monstrosity.

In 1825 William Lloyd Garrison completed his typesetting apprenticeship in Boston. With his shirt collar unbuttoned in the manner of Lord Byron, he dreamed of sailing off to fight with the Greeks for their freedom. But because he suffered from seasickness, he spared himself the long voyage and stuck around, only to be moved by Walker's *Appeal*, and he became one of the greatest antiracists of his (or any) time, proving that not all white men are monsters!

The American working class of the time was organized around color: red, white, and black. An Egyptian army of six thousand soldiers invaded Greece in 1824 on behalf of the Ottoman Empire, and this army included many people described as "Negroes," who roundly defeated the ill-organized Greeks and enslaved those whom they did not kill. Lord Byron led a small band of fighters—two hundred, according to some estimates—as well as many black women who'd been tasked with caretaking them as laundresses and cooks.

---

23 Peter P. Hinks, *To Awaken My Afflicted Brethren: David Walker and the Problem of Antebellum Slave-Resistance* (University Park: Pennsylvania State University Press, 1997), 199.

Byron himself was chauffeured by a black West Indian named Benjamin Lewis, who was the poet's groom and responsible for the care of his team of horses. Lewis befriended two black women who had been slaves of the Turks, but who had been liberated and were now starving. He begged for Byron's help. "My determination," said Byron, "is that the children born of these black women, of which you may be the father, shall be my property, and I will maintain them."[24] Although a martyr to Greek freedom, how can we claim that this Romantic hero was an abolitionist of slavery?

Elijah McCoy (1843–1929) helped to grease the wheels of industry and then to sprinkle the lawns of suburbia. A conductor on the Underground Railroad, he used the space beneath the false bottom of his wagon to transport fugitive slaves to Wyandotte, from whence they were ferried over the river to Canada. His parents had fled the slave state of Kentucky by crossing the Ohio River. On their way to Canada they passed through and then later returned to Ypsilanti. McCoy spent five years as an engineer's apprentice in Edinburgh, Scotland; he too returned to Ypsi, and in 1872 took out a patent for an Automatic Steam Chest Locomotive Lubrication Device. Discerning engineers called this device "The Real McCoy," while the rest referred to it as a lubrication cup. Thus Elijah McCoy oiled trains that hauled the coal and iron that together formed the foundations of industrial civilization. What was his role in the railway strikes of the 1880s? Eugene V. Debs, a locomotive man, union organizer, and socialist, united the engine drivers and the brakemen. When the powers-that-be tried to shift labor's holiday from May 1 into September, Eugene Debs came to its defense. "This

---

24 Fiona McCarthy, *Byron: Life and Legend* (New York: Farrar, Straus and Giroux, 2002), 507. European racial slavery begins with the Romany people, or Gypsies.

is the first and only International Labor Day. It belongs to the working class and is dedicated to the revolution."[25]

As for reproduction, we remember Elijah McCoy for his lawn sprinkler patent. Following the destruction of the prairie, the sprinkler became a necessary item for the prettification of the suburban front lawns of the 1950s, when ticky-tacky houses for nuclear families were all the rage. McCoy died irritable and irascible. We might more easily remember his wife, Mary, who wrote an appeal against lynching: "Justice, where art thou? Thou Church of the Living God, why slumberest thou? Awake! Awake! and hear Ethiopia's cry for her people!"[26] Like David Walker or Percy Shelley, Mary McCoy prophesied by hurling anathemas at bloodsuckers in a voice intended to awaken the dead.

Let us follow her forward. She resisted the terrorism of the monstrous regime of labor created a hundred years earlier, at the beginning of the industrial-mechanical transformation. Death by lynching or execution reduces the value of life to point zero. Its exploitation depends, as we see in both *Frankenstein* and *The Vampyre*, upon dead labor. Now that we have addressed the losses of blood, names, and the commons, we may turn to the beautiful promise of May.

The Green . . .
Approaching Ypsilanti from the west, one passes the notoriously phallic water tower and is reminded of the traditional rhyme,

> Hooray! Hooray! The First of May!
> Outdoor f***ing begins today!

---

25 Philip S. Foner, *May Day: A Short History of the International Workers' Holiday* (New York: International Publishers, 1986), 77.

26 Albert P. Marshall, *The "Real McCoy" of Ypsilanti* (Ypsilanti: Marlan, 1989), 23.

Across the globe people celebrate the arrival of spring, with its "fructifying spirit of vegetation." We do this in May, which takes its name from Maia, who in Greek mythology is a mother of gods. The Greeks had sacred groves, the Druids worshipped oaks, and the Romans played games in honor of Floralia. In Scotland, herdsfolk formed circles and danced around fires. Celts lit bonfires on hilltops to honor Beltane, their own god. In the Tyrol, people encouraged their dogs to bark and made music with pots and pans. In Scandinavia fires were built and out came witches.

The world over, people went a-Maying. They went into the woods and returned with leaf, bough, and blossom, with which to garland their bodies, homes, and loved ones. Acts of theatre featuring characters like "Jack-in-the-Green" and the "Queen of the May" were performed out of doors. Trees were planted and Maypoles erected. There was dancing, music, drinking, and lovemaking. Winter was over. Spring had sprung.

In Wallachia and Moldavia, home to Dracula as well as to those rulers from whom the city of Ypsilanti takes its name, there was a May spirit. Emily Gerard, an English folklorist who tramped through the region in the 1870s, describes it: "The *Gana* is the name of a beautiful but malicious witch who presides over the evil spirits holding their meetings on the eve of the 1st of May. *Gana* is said to have been the mistress of Transylvania before the Christian era. Her beauty bewitched many, but whoever succumbed to her charms, and let himself be lured into quaffing mead from her ure-ox drinking horn, was doomed."

Despite its complexities, whether May Day has been observed by sacred or profane ritual, by pagans or by Christian, Muslim, or Jewish monotheists, by magic or not, by straights or gays, by gentle or calloused hands, it has always been a celebration of all that is free, green, and life-giving in the world. Whatever it was, it was not a workday, and therefore was attacked by those in power.

. . . and the Red

Don't be bamboozled about the Red May Day: it began here in America. There are two essential stories about this; one is Merry Mount and the other, Haymarket.

Let's begin with Merry Mount. Gloomy Puritans wanted to isolate themselves ("the city on the hill") and, having accepted the hospitality of native peoples, proceeded to wage war against them and to make them sick. Thomas Morton, on the other hand, arrived in 1624 and desired to work, trade, and enjoy life with the natives. He envisioned a life based on abundance rather than scarcity, and three years later he celebrated May Day with a giant Maypole: "a goodly pine tree of eighty feet long was reared up, with a pair of buckhorns nailed on somewhat near unto the top of it." William Bradford, who landed the *Mayflower* in Massachusetts, thought Indians were agents of the Antichrist. Of Thomas Morton and his crew, Bradford wrote in total disgust that "they also set up a maypole and dancing about it many days together, inviting the Indian women for their consorts, dancing and frisking together like so many fairies, or furies, rather, and worse practices. [It was] as if they had anew revived the celebrated feasts of the Roman goddess Flora, or the beastly practices of the mad Bacchanalians." Myles Standish destroyed Merry Mount, as Morton's commune was called, and in so doing brought America's first Red May Day to a bloody end. Despite this, we remember Flora, the frisky fairies, and the beastly practitioners.

And we remember Haymarket. The movement for an eight-hour workday began at the conclusion of the civil war that abolished slavery. Ira Steward of the International

Workingmen's Association, along with the National Labor Union, called for it. The American Federation of Labor (A.F. of L.) resolved in 1884 "that eight hours shall constitute a legal day's labor from May First, 1886 . . ."

> We want to feel the sunshine;
> We want to smell the flowers.
> We're sure God has willed it.
> And we mean to have eight hours.
>
> We're summoning our forces from
> Shipyard, shop and mill;
> Eight hours for work, eight hours for rest,
> Eight hours for what we will.

Work—Rest—Play: it's a persuasive program, is it not?

Accordingly, a huge march was held in Chicago on May Day in 1886. Ironworkers of the Molder's Union struck at the McCormick Reaper Works in Chicago. Police killed some of the workers, and to protest their murders a meeting was called for May 4 at Haymarket Square. Militant workers and armed police faced off, a stick of dynamite was thrown (nobody knows by whom), and all hell broke loose. Sam Fielden, August Spies, Albert Parsons, Oscar Neebe, Michael Schwab, Adolph Fischer, George Engel, and Louis Lingg were found guilty in a spectacularly unfair trial. Four of them were hanged on November 11, 1887, despite an international campaign against the trial's injustice. The way was thus prepared for the Gilded Age of American capitalism, and May Day became a day of workers' solidarity everywhere in the world *except* the United States. We have been bamboozled.

Now that we know, we shall not forget.

Whereas Green celebrations were carnivalesque and temporarily turned the world's economic classes and power relations upside down, Red demonstrations sought to turn May Day into a revolution that had the abolition of the class system as its aim. While the Red and the Green stand together in opposition to avarice and privatization, there are ways in which they differ. Green May Day is related to the realm of the commons (the location of subsistence on the ground), while Red May Day is related to the public sphere (formed in relation to institutions of the state). The commons tend to be invisible until taken away, while the public realm is all too visible as a spectacle of not much more than purchase and sale. An Ypsi man named Oakley Johnson was both: a Green commoner and a Red revolutionary.

Oakley Johnson Learns "Take It Easy"

Oakley Johnson was born in 1890 in a log cabin in Arenac County, Michigan. He split wood, speared fish, and fell asleep at night to the sound of bullfrogs and whip-poor-wills. At school he read Aesop, ancient history, and Darwin. He attended Baptist, Methodist, and Congregational churches, but after reading Tom Paine and Colonel Ingersoll ("the great agnostic") he began to doubt that "Jesus was the *only* son of God," and was asked not to return to Bible class.

Johnson had learned "The Deserted Village," Oliver Goldsmith's long poem about the ruling-class theft of English and Irish common lands. Goldsmith (1730–74) was Irish and had investigated the matter.

> Ill fares the land, to hastening ills a prey,
> Where wealth accumulates and men decay.

Debilitation, drunkenness, and depression awaited the 99 percent. As for the 1 percent,

> The man of wealth and pride,
> Takes up a space that many poor supplied;

> Space for his lake, his park's extended bounds,
> Space for his horses, equipage, and hounds;
> The robe that wraps his limbs in silken cloth,
> Has robbed the neighboring fields of half their growth.

Not only did the wealthy landowner wrest away communal lands and sculpt them into picturesque views, he also monopolized the game (rabbits, pheasants, deer) and raised rents in order to be able to purchase his luxuries.

> Those fenceless fields the sons of wealth divide,
> And even the bare-worn commons is denied.

And if the commoners objected, as frequently they did by rioting, poaching, and even playing football, the terrorism of capital punishment might await them.

> While the proud their long-drawn pomps display,
> There the black gibbet glooms beside the way.

Surely Oakley compared his remarkable achievement of memory (it is a *long* poem!) to his own life-experience, which included time spent in an Ojibwa village near Harbor Springs. There he would have thought about the commons, which at that moment was the subject of worldwide conversation. In 1912 he attended what is now Ferris State University, where he became a revolutionary socialist.

In Davenport, Iowa, he attended Industrial Workers of the World ("Wobbly") street meetings, and got to know Frank Little, whom he asked about sabotage. "We don't advocate destruction of the products of our labor, that would be folly," said Little, whose mother was Native American. "But if conditions don't permit us to quit work, we can work more slowly, can't we? That would be striking on the job. The workers of Europe call this 'Ca Canny,' or 'Take it easy.' If the bosses refuse to pay us a full day's wage, why should we give them a full day's work?" In 1995 Ypsilanti became the headquarters of the IWW, with an office at 103 West Michigan Avenue.

Frank Little was lynched in Butte, Montana, in 1917 by agents of the copper bosses. Johnson signed up for his red card, and attended the Michigan State Normal School, which still stands opposite the water tower and the white marble bust of Demetrios Ypsilantis. Johnson then took a position as a principal at Grant High School in Ypsilanti. Midway through the school year, Johnson was yanked out of his classroom by representatives of the U.S. Department of Justice, who removed him to Grand Rapids in order to interrogate him about his nationality and to learn why he had contributed money to a legal defense fund established for Wobblies who were undergoing prosecution. Johnson refused to be bullied, and the following day he called a school assembly at which he recounted the entire story.

"From that day, the atmosphere changed," Johnson later recalled.

> The students and the farmers round about were on my side. In June, on the day before graduation, an out-of-town mob gathered at the school house to get me, but my students spirited me and my young wife out the back way, where farmers in automobiles rescued us and gave us hospitality for the night. The next day Professor Hoyt of Ypsilanti gave the graduating address, and expressed regret, I was told, that the mob on the preceding night had to go home empty handed. My graduating class refused to sit on the platform because I was not there. They picked up their diplomas later, after the "exercises" were over.

In October of 1920 Johnson starting teaching at the University of Michigan, where he remained until 1928.

May Day 1934 and the Curriculum

On May Day in 1934, on the front cover of its journal the *New Masses*, the Communist Party in America issued a poetic call by "Joe Hill" author Alfred Hayes:

> Into the streets May First!
> Into the roaring Square!

Hayes casts his gaze back to Haymarket Square. For us the "roaring Square" is an analog of Cairo's Tahrir Square, where people set in motion the momentous events of 2011, which in turn flowered into such phenomena as Occupy Ypsilanti. Hayes was calling people to march to Union Square in Manhattan.

> Shake the midtown towers!
> Shatter the downtown air!

We remember and mourn the loss of three thousand fellow workers in the World Trade Center catastrophe of 2001.

> Come with a storm of banners,
> Come with an earthquake tread,
> Bells, hurl out of your belfries,
> Red flag, leap out your red!
> Out of the shops and factories,
> Up with the sickle and hammer,
> Comrades, these are our tools,
> A song and a banner!

The hammer and sickle represented the alliance of industry and agriculture, or wageworkers and peasants.

> Roll song, from the sea of our hearts,
> Banner, leap and be free;
> Song and banner together,
> Down with the bourgeoisie!

We hurl the bright bomb of the sun,
The moon like a hand grenade.

This poem was composed well before Hiroshima, Nagasaki, Three Mile Island, Chernobyl, and Fukushima.

Pour forth like a second flood!
Thunder the alps of the air!
Subways are roaring our millions—
Comrades, into the Square!

Despite its limitations, this attempt to compare the energy of the 99 percent to sublime terrestrial and cosmic forces should be a challenge to our own movement and its creativity. In Egypt, Madrid, and Oakland, how can we translate the energy of the square into the beauty of the circle?

In the same issue of the *New Masses*, Oakley Johnson published two articles concerning "Education Under the Crisis." He described how thousands of PhDs were looking for work, thousands of college teachers were laid off, and thousands of students who "normally" work their way through college could not do so; many who formerly paid tuition had nothing to pay with. He wrote, "*there are no jobs…*" Tuition was raised by 25 percent at Columbia. White-collar workers—chemists, engineers, accountants, physicians—were also without work.

The people yearned to comprehend their economic situation; they were thirsty for knowledge in general. Book circulation jumped from thirty-three million to forty-three million in one year alone, while education budgets were reduced from $11.5 million to $8 million. Langston Hughes castigated the leaders of Negro colleges for reactionary policies, and half of the teachers at those institutions believed in the notion of the inherent inferiority of African Americans. Furthermore, graduate student assistants were expected to work "*for nothing.*"

Administrators believed that "education" could be a palliative to the injuries caused by economic disaster, that it could treat the depressed as if it were no more than Valium, Prozac, or Wellbutrin. Even the "starving poor" were expected to go to night school and passively ingest self-help classes. College deans and presidents advised unemployed PhDs to lead discussion groups and nature hikes for Boy Scouts. Medical schools weeded out any applicant who lacked a "gracious personality." They were fearful of the "new leisure"; idle people should have hobbies. In Lansing, a "People's University" was organized by the YMCA; its instructors were businessmen, and its meetings took place at a bank. Students empowering themselves on picket lines? Satisfying their hunger at integrated lunch counters? Cutting class in order to march on May Day? Blacks and whites dancing together? No, no, no, and no!

"The gigantic attack on the colleges," Johnson wrote, "made under cover of the 'depression,' is in fact an attack upon intellectuals as a class,—an attack upon middle class professional and white collar workers. It is an attempt not only to reduce the standard of living of teacher-intellectuals, but to reduce the overproduction of intellectuals by striking at higher education.... Students and teachers and professional workers must resist the attack. Particularly must college teachers, last to wake up and last to act, organize for struggle."

In an earlier article, "A Five-Inch Shelf of Booklets," Johnson had tried to fashion a revolutionary answer to Harvard University President Charles William Eliot's philhellenist bamboozlement in *The Harvard Classics*. Theoretical writing requires study, and Johnson warned that "the inquiring and newly radicalized intellectual must watch his step." His study of political economy is essential to this inquiry and should not be postponed. Johnson recommended *Socialism: Utopian and Scientific* by Friedrich Engels, a work which featured an essay on the commons ("The Mark"). He also suggested the study of Alexander Trachtenberg's *History of May Day*, and Lenin's *Imperialism*, itself sorely in need of a revival.

Bob Marley also debamboozled the issue:

> De Babylon system is the vampire, falling empire,
> Suckin' the blood of the sufferers,
> Building church and university,
> Deceiving the people continually.

Between 1923 and 1928 the Negro-Caucasian Club met in Ann Arbor, at the University of Michigan. Oakley Johnson, then a teacher of English literature and of rhetoric at the university, was the club's faculty sponsor as well as the chaperone at its dances. With his wife he hosted the group in their home. The club was started by Lenoir Smith, a student from Mississippi; another early leader was a young West Indian man by the name of Fairclough. One day, following an all-nighter and a morning hectic with lectures, exams, and papers, Smith went out for a quick lunch, and in the midst of her fatigue was stunned to be refused service at the lunch counter. The club came to her aid and held a sit-in at the restaurant. Was it the first of its kind? Shall Ann Arbor, led by Ypsilantian Oakley Johnson, claim priority in the lunch counter sit-in movement?

The group also attempted to integrate college dances, as well as the university swimming pool and gymnasium, but without success. The dean—who was "more than hostile" and boasted that his grandfather had owned slaves in Virginia—insisted that "the name of the University not be used in connection with the activities of the Negro-Caucasian Club."[27]

---

27   *Negro History Bulletin* 33, no. 2 (February 1970) or the *Michigan Quarterly Review* (Spring 1969). See also, "Trying to Live 'Really Human,'" an autobiographical typescript written by Oakley Johnson for his

The guest speakers the club brought to town included Alain Locke, W.E.B. Du Bois, Jean Toomer, and Clarence Darrow.

Willow Run and the Birth of Ypsitucky

Ypsilanti is sometimes called Ypsitucky. Here's why.

Willow Run was built in 1940 and became the biggest factory in the world; it was a mile in length, and produced a bomber an hour. A quarter of a million people moved into southeast Michigan, "some tens of thousands of hillbillies, CIO unionists, and transients from the ends of the continent." Ford recruited from Tennessee and Kentucky, establishing in "Ypsitucky" a cultural divide within its working class. At its peak in 1943 it employed more than forty thousand workers. Although there were fifty-six showers available at the factory, no provision was made for worker housing. Here was a crisis of both production *and* reproduction.

Warren Kidder was expropriated at Willow Run.

"Government conscription of our land . . . forced us off the farm . . ." With the roar of bulldozers echoing in his ears, the barn was burnt, the woods were cleared, and the tree stumps left in place. "The horrors of what was happening to me and to my family left scars and hidden forces below the surface of the land and in my mind that even time would never cease."

Harry Bennett was Ford's pistol-packing director of personnel. He ruled "with his collection of Purple Gang mobsters and political fixers" and instilled terror throughout the hierarchy of Ford management.[28] His "theory of supervision" consisted of the belief "the worker is never right." Armed

---

grandchildren, located in a folder marked "Other Papers" in Box 2 of the Johnson Papers, Labadie Collection, University of Michigan.

28 Warren Benjamin Kidder, *Willow Run: Colossus of American Industry* (1995), 39–41. The Purple Gang muscled in on labor as it had during the Cleaners and Dyers War of 1927.

guards oversaw production in factories that suffered high turnover (at a rate, in some years, of as much as 100 percent). Among the top complaints of the factory workers was that there was "No Place to Stay," even, in some cases, after having worked at the factory for years; another complaint was "Ran Out of Money."[29] Theft of tools was another problem (how to build a shack?), as was absenteeism (and when to build it?).

This insufficiency of worker housing resulted in "the worst mess in the whole United States." The housing that did exist was lousy: tents, tarpaper shacks, or trailers with outdoor toilets. "Unless the husband had built a vestibule,—prohibited in government camps—muddy shoes and rubbers tracked good old Michigan mud into the living room after every rain—spring, summer, fall, or winter. It was always wash day for trailer wives and mothers."[30] A woman's work was never done.

The government solution to this housing shortage was to construct the first "free way" (toll-less government road) in the United States. An automobile commute enabled the workers to live as far away from their jobs as Detroit, for instance.

Rosie the Riveter, a phantom composite who proliferated in song and print, was in fact a representation of millions of women.[31] In 1942 Betty Oelke, an eighteen-year-old, newly married farmgirl, traded a dress for slacks, punched a clock and went to work. She stood on her feet nine hours a day, six days a week, building bombers at the Willow Run plant. "I'd drill all day, and another girl would put the rivets in," she said. The work was repetitive and her bosses were

---

29 Lowell Carr and James Stermer, *Willow Run* (New York: Harper, 1952), 9, 36, 104, 208.

30 Kidder, *Willow Run*, 184.

31 Ypsilanti Historical Society archives. Willow Run Collection, "Rosie the Riveter" file.

male and mean. "They would stand right there and time you." In hindsight she acknowledged, "it was the beginning of women's liberation."

Women's liberation would take some time—two or three decades. Meanwhile, right after the war, women were expelled from the factories, and a process of racial segregation was developed in the housing policies of Willow Village. A 1967 report by Alan Haber to the federal government stated that the black community suffered from "hate and self-hate, apathy, hostility and hopelessness, dead-end jobs, and a family and community life barren of the enrichments and varied opportunities for pleasure and growth that are taken for granted in the affluent, white community. The whites, too, are often deformed by racism, identifying the Negroes as an enemy group, which threatened their status, security, and physical welfare."

A golf course divided the white community from the black. In 1965 a community action project had been designed to mobilize poor people on their own behalf, "with maximum feasible participation," as was the phrase of the day. It failed. The report reached two remarkable conclusions to account for this failure. First, "there was almost no 'utopian thinking,'" and second, "the project lacked a sense of history."[32] These words were written almost fifty years ago, and anticipate both Howard Zinn's people's history project as well as our Occupy Wall Street–inspired dreams.

X²: Or, a Theoretical Excursus

We began by invoking two horror stories that were conceived at a moment of world crisis. One of them led us to the name

---

32 Alan Haber, *The Community Organization Approach to Anti-poverty Action: An Evaluation of the Willow Village Project*, Report to the Office of Economic Opportunity (typescript, University of Michigan, 1967), 53, 313, 315.

of Ypsilanti and helped us to develop an international perspective. Both stories contribute to our understanding of two malignant structures of social life: first, the utter destructiveness of capitalism to body and soul, and, second, the monstrosity of racism. The former drains the body of life and the latter perverts the soul. If we could return to the structures of thinking of the peasant cultures whence the vampire story originates, the solution to its evil appears magically: garlic, or a stake in the heart. We might even dream up symbolic meanings to these ancient remedies. The spirit of May Day, however, requires that we take practical steps.

What is the relation between the bulldozers destroying homes at Willow Run and the construction of the world's largest factory? What is the relationship between Goldsmith's deserted village in Ireland, the Indian village of Sanscrainte, and the Communist proletarians of 1934? What's the relationship between the golf course in Benton Harbor and economic austerity in Ypsilanti? And what of loss of fuel rights in Transylvania and the expansion of slavery in the United States? Here we find a morasse of bamboozlement!

What is the relation between the loss of our commons—their *expropriation*, so often achieved, according to the Moor, via letters of blood and fire, which for us means drones, structural adjustment programs, invasions, civil wars, "sectarian" violence, "ethnic" violence, and school-closings, factory-closings, foreclosures, and enclosures—and the subsequent cuts to our social wages and institutions? Our schools, libraries, health clinics, city parks, medical insurance, and jobs have been knifed. With the expansion of mandatory overtime and the contraction of our vacations, our workdays and workloads—our working lives!—are lengthened.

I call this phenomenon "X squared," to show that *expropriation* compounds *exploitation*. For economist David Harvey, X^2 means "exploitation by dispossession." If you refuse to abide by this criminal racket (cunningly referred to as "entre-preneurship") what awaits you is wage-stagnation, poverty, or prison.

How might we relate X^2 to the crises of production and reproduction? Expropriation, as we have seen, refers to the theft of our commons and common goods. Our reproduction depends upon common land as well as the *action* of common-ing. Even government-as-commoning has been possible, as Nobel laureate Elinor Ostrom has shown. When all is said and done, however, the solution to our crisis of reproduction is to discover and then reclaim our commons.

You don't need to be an avid follower of the Occupy movement to know that in Washtenaw County the crises in housing and education are on everyone's mind. Foreclosure is expropriation, while higher education fees and the massive student debt they incur constitute exploitation. In Ypsilanti, school district budget overruns coupled with diminishing state funding for education mean the imminent appoint-ment of an emergency financial manager. The housing crisis results in such things as Camp Take Notice, a homeless tent community outside Ann Arbor, a city whose own Occupy group has devoted its energies to the establishment of a twenty-four-hour, seven-days-a-week "warming center" for the shivering homeless. This initiative failed, as did plans to establish a commons on top of the multistory underground parking structure next to the downtown branch of the Ann Arbor Public Library.

The creature produced by the technocrat Dr. Frankenstein wandered all over the face of the earth, without any regard for national borders. Likewise, the vampire ignores national, sexual, and racial differences so long as the blood is red! Capitalist hunger for surplus value is inter-national and achieves its exsanguinary goals by relocating plants, equipment, genes, data, and people as it pleases. When the International Monetary Fund met in October of 2011 in Nafplion, the trade unions organized a huge demonstration against it under the following banner:

YOUR WEALTH, OUR BLOOD!

Bloodsuckers are international, but then so are we, if we only . . .

AWAKEN! AROUSE! ARISE! OCCUPY FOR MAY DAY

Bloodsucking is not only symbolic. Around the corner from the University of Toledo, where I work, are three shops that share a parking lot: a plasma shop, a check-cashing store, and a liquor store. They've stayed put, and have apparently prospered, while many university presidents have come and gone, and they conveniently enable that patently American life cycle whereby a man sells his blood, cashes his check, and then gets plastered.

The land of zombies! Home of the undead. Oh, shame!

The dictator Sulla was wholly bent on slaughter and no sanctuary of the gods, hearth of hospitality, or ancestral home could defend against his wrath. But Sulla came to a bloody end too. According to Plutarch's *Lives*, it went something like this: his bowels were ulcerated ("his very meat was polluted") and even his skin attracted lice, which no amount of picking or bathing could destroy. Having been told that a magistrate had allowed someone to defer the payment of a public debt, Sulla berated the man and then had him strangled. But his screaming and exertion were too great a strain on him, and with "the imposthume [abscess or cyst] breaking, he lost a great quantity of blood" and died. Even though, as David Graeber reminds us, credit and debt have always been backed by violence, it is rare for a dictator's days to conclude so poetically, expiring by his own medicine.[33] Remember Sulla!

"And forgive us our debts, as we forgive our debtors," advised a carpenter's son. Let us also remember David Walker, Karl Marx, Mary McCoy, and Albert Parsons.

And let us not forget Howard Zinn, Oakley Johnson, Mary Shelley, and Reverend Pinkney.

There will be a test!

Let us not forget the English romantics, the Chicago anarchists, or the New York Communists. We brought an end to one kind of slavery: plantation racial slavery. We brought an end to one kind of capital punishment: lynching by mobs. Can we bring to an end the vampirine dictatorships of corporations and their emergency managers? Or do we simply mourn the eight-hour workday and our commons as dead and gone?

There will be a test!

Though we are the 99 percent, few Americans identify as "working class": in our country this term has been seriously compromised, despite the fact that the world is yearning for a solidarity that might overthrow the princes, modern-day hospodars, CEOs, Caesars and Sullas, emergency managers, and the rest of the 1 percent. More of us are proletarian—lacking the means of subsistence—than ever before.

May Day is the day we perceive anew who we are and what we want. We dissolve the "I" into the "we" on this glorious and revolutionary day of unity, and by our words and actions we decide what kind of union we desire to build. Trade union, craft union, industrial union, marriage union, family union, national and tribal union, one big union, or even class union: these are our unions of production and

---

33 David Graeber, *Debt: The First 5,000 Years* (Brooklyn: Melville House, 2011).

reproduction. May 1 is a practical day; we discover who are our brothers and sisters, and in so doing we forge solidarity. This is how we create the future: with collectivity and cooperation.

What are our responsibilities this May Day? We must preserve the General Assemblies of the 99 percent. Together we must occupy common space, and what better spaces to inhabit than the squares, parks, halls, streets, libraries, factories, schools, and plazas which have been privatized or simply abandoned? And what about the stolen-land-turned-golf-course in Benton Harbor? We should fill the streets and make our presences known to one another by sight, sound, and touch. We are Many, they are Few.

We must have a Maypole. We must preserve Ypsilanti's public assets. We must fill the streets so that we may actually see we are the 99 percent. We must welcome fellow creatures who are undocumented. We must drive a stake through the heart of the monstrosity of white supremacy. We must avoid dictatorship even as it masquerades under pseudonym. We must envision for our children a future without prison. We must debamboozle what is offered to them in school. We must turn brownfields green. We must reclaim our commons and create new ones. None can accomplish this alone. Let us vouchsafe to ourselves that together in common we can, if we only

AWAKEN! AROUSE! ARISE!
OCCUPY FOR MAY DAY!

Further Reading

Boal, Iain, Janferie Stone, Michael Watts, and Cal Winslow, eds. *West of Eden: Communes and Utopia in Northern California*. Oakland: PM Press, 2012.

Brecher, Jeremy. *Strike!* Oakland: PM Press, 2014.

Caffentzis, George. "On the Notion of a Crisis of Social Reproduction: A Theoretical Review." In *Women, Development and Labor of Reproduction: Struggles and Movements*, edited by Mariarosa Dalla Costa and Giovanna F. Dalla Costa. Trenton, NJ: Africa World Press, 1999, 153–87.

Federici, Silvia. *Revolution at Point Zero: Housework, Reproduction, and Feminist Struggle*. Oakland: PM Press, 2012.

Graeber, David. *Debt: The First 5,000 Years*. Brooklyn: Melville House, 2011.

Green, James. *Death in the Haymarket: A Story of Chicago, the First Labor Movement, and the Bombing that Divided Gilded Age America*. New York: Pantheon Books, 2006.

Harvey, David. *The New Imperialism*. Oxford: Oxford University Press, 2003.

Hawthorne, Nathaniel. "The Maypole of Merry Mount." In *Twice-Told Tales*. Boston: American Stationers Co., 1837.

Linebaugh, Peter. *The Magna Carta Manifesto: Liberties and Commons for All*. Berkeley: University of California Press, 2008.

Marsh, George Perkins. *Man and Nature; or, Physical Geography as Modified by Human Action*. New York: Charles Scribner, 1864.

Marx, Karl. *Capital: A Critique of Political Economy*. Vol. 1. Translated by Ben Fowkes. London: Penguin Books, 1976.

McNally, David. *Monsters of the Market: Zombies, Vampires and Global Capitalism*. Historical Materialism Book Series, Vol. 30. Leiden, Netherlands: Brill, 2011.

Morton, Thomas. *The New English Canaan*. London, 1637.

Rosemont, Franklin, and David Roediger, eds. *The Haymarket Scrapbook*. Chicago and Oakland: Charles Kerr and AK Press, 2012.

Stoker, Bram. *Dracula* (1897). Edited by Nina Auerbach and David J. Skal. New York: W.W. Norton & Co., 1997.

Trachtenberg, Alexander. *History of May Day*. New York: International Publishers, 1947.

Vradis, Antonis, and Dimitris Dalakoglou, eds. *Revolt and Crisis in Greece: Between a Present Yet to Pass and a Future Still to Come*. Oakland and London: AK Press and Occupied London, 2011.

Walker, David. *Appeal to the Coloured Citizens of the World* (1829). Edited by Peter P. Hinks. University Park: Pennsylvania State University Press, 2000.

Zinn, Howard. *A People's History of the United States*. New York: Harper & Row, 1980.

ELEVEN

Swan Honk May Day

How Did We Get Here (University Hall) at
This Point of Time (the "Anthropocene")?

(2014)

These reflections originate in rage. True, I have accepted the wisdom of AA that righteous anger is better left to others, like Dylan Thomas who rages against the dying of the light, or like William Blake's tigers of wrath. Still, I must put into words what I feel and the causes of those feelings.

I was going to say don't worry, but in light of my conclusion, which recommends revolution by the workers of the world, I can't advise that because success is by no means sure. There's plenty to worry about but not me having a fit!

My rage is not the kind that can be mollified by a pill or therapy. The *Oxford English Dictionary* gives one of the meanings of "rage" as poetic or prophetic enthusiasm.

You know the second edition of the *Oxford English Dictionary* contains more than 2,400,000 quotations from literature and conversation to illustrate the meanings of words. Under each word these quotations are arranged chronologically. Thus you get a history of every word's meanings and how it changes. The *OED* was first titled the *New English Dictionary on Historical Principles* (1884–1928).

The preface explains, "though it deals primarily with words, it is virtually an encyclopedic treasury of information about things." English language(s) are great sources of historical evidence. I'll come back to *OED* at the end of my lecture.

But now, back to rage. It presented itself as self-willed isolation as I tried to blend into the institution. The rage is dull, even numb, as if it could not recognize itself. There is something slavish about it. I've been here twenty years. Twenty years a slave? The judgment seems excessively harsh but consider:

I used to walk from Tucker Hall to University Hall every spring just as the magnolias were blooming to talk to the dean. I had to beg for summer teaching. I needed the money for the August mortgage. Every dean said, Sorry, can't help. One, in an embarrassing intrusion into my private life, advised that I do my budgeting better, another with hard-headed, neoliberal realism said that I should go on the "job market" to get a better offer.

These slights are part of a whole and the whole consists of devaluation. In rank I am the worst paid member of the faculty.

In 1997 I brought two artists over from England, equally brilliant as poets, dramatists, and musicians, to perform a play about James Aitken. Have you heard of him? In 1776 on behalf of American liberty he set fire to the ropewalks in the dockyards of Portsmouth, England. The Americans won independence because of the inferiority of English ships. Literally he carried the torch of liberty.

No one came to the play.

Something was wrong, we weren't working together, people forgot what revolution is about, even their own.

The university found my department sexist, or deficient in its number and treatment of women. I agreed and said so. Some of the men in the department wanted to argue with me. But what would you think if you were mocked at a departmental meeting for requesting that the gentlemen using the common bathrooms first raise the seat?

Rage is related to shame, I can tell you.

The historians have been reduced from more than twenty tenured or tenure-track positions when I joined in 1994 to now two tenured in 2014. The College of Liberal Arts has been abolished.

The *OED* has been removed from the ground floor of the library where I could quickly check something before class. Carlson Library has been stripped of about half its books. Actually they don't say stripped. One library worker called it "a culling." Their word of choice was "weeding." This happened around the time, 2011, that the billionaire Bloomberg cleared out the five thousand volumes of the People's Library of Zuccotti Park by scooping them up in sanitation trucks in the dark of night and dumping the books into the Hudson River. Bloomberg called it "cleaning."

Weeding, culling, cleaning: at least it wasn't burning. Here's Heinrich Heine writing in 1821,

. . . wo man Bücher verbrennt
Verbrennt man
Auch am Ende Menschen

"Where people start by burning books they end up by burning people." No, the ovens haven't been fired up yet, but devaluation by other means is rampant and spreading.

If you are a scholar or a teacher this is an expropriation. More teaching, fewer books. This is what Marx meant when he said workers become proletarians when they lose the means of production. While some professors still flatter themselves that we are not proles, we live now in a kind of scholarly PTSD.

Last week the library closed because the sewers backed up. I couldn't have chosen a better metaphor for my retirement if I'd tried.

Remember John Milton (*Areopagitica* 1644): "Books are not absolutely dead things. . . . I know they are as lively, and as vigorously productive, as those fabulous dragon's teeth; and being sown up and down, may chance to spring up armed men."

This was a working-class university, "for Toledo's working boys and girls," as Abdul Alkalimat discovered in the language of one of the early university charters. The university in the United States has become a debt machine; it mediates the transfer of a trillion dollars from students to banks and consigns the students to a lifetime of indentured servitude.

To sum up. We have lost faculty, we have lost our college, we have lost our building, we have lost books, and we have lost our value; we have been devalued. I mentioned this to the public librarian in Ypsilanti, and she reminded me, "Peter, this is the story of every working-class person."

Precisely.

UT has become a business university, or a corporate university, in its values, in its personnel, in its hierarchies, and in its finances. The rage originates not just in twenty years of teaching at the University of Toledo. The rage has been smoldering for over fifty years of teaching in U.S. academia.

In 1970 I was at the University of Warwick, UK, which was beholden to the auto business of its environs. E.P. Thompson, the historian of the working class, called it a business university and asked, "Is it inevitable that the university will be reduced to the function of providing, with increasingly authoritarian efficiency, pre-packed intellectual commodities which meet the requirement of management? Or can we by our efforts transform it into a centre of free discussion and action, tolerating and even encouraging 'subversive' thought and activity for a dynamic renewal of the whole society within which it operates?"[1]

---

1   E.P. Thompson, *Warwick University Ltd.: Industry, Management and the Universities* (1970; repr., Nottingham: Spokesman, 2014), 166.

The cause of the rage is general. It is directed against capitalism and imperialism. The unbelievable betrayals that began as anger against specific offenses such as Jim Crow and the Vietnam War have only grown into a vast hidden rage. The Black Power and Third World uprisings; the explosion in the auto plants; the abolition of patriarchy, but not the end of the glass ceiling. By equality we meant equality of conditions, not equality of opportunity, because opportunity is for opportunists. What is the human race if not equality?

The rage arises from the enormous prison gulag-leviathan that squats over the country in an obscene and hypocritical extension of the old slave regime. Six million are under correctional supervision. Six times as much money is spent on prisons as on education.

The corporate university is joined at the hip to the military. The spirit of the one is to question authority; but the spirit of the other is to obey it.

Even the military presence is privatized: The soldiers and veterans are honored by corporations who no longer guise themselves as the "public" or the "country." Just look at the sponsoring names on the memorial between U Hall and the Field House!

Why is there not a single public bench, not to mention a building, a statue, or a portrait of Scott and Helen Nearing? Nearing was brought in by Tucker (among others) as dean of the college. He opposed the war in 1917; he started a women's studies program, until the combined forces of the Chamber of Commerce, the Catholic Church, and the Bureau of Investigation fired him. What a disgrace!

Now it is worse. The planet suffers, the air is going, the waters are going. The planet's lands have become a sewer, its waters a sink. Now it means beryllium under the children's playground; it means plastic bottles clog up the

Pacific Ocean; suffocating algae blooms in the lakes; it means choking CO_2 in the sky. The "sixth extinction" is upon us.

The rage came out of silence. It came from self-repression. The rage fills me with loathing; it affects the psyche; it affects the family. It was caused by the failure to bring about a revolution for a new society, a working-class revolution against capitalism and imperialism. What could these terms mean? Are they just rhetoric? This is the rage.

This is my last chance at UT to explain, to say my piece. How did we get here, University Hall?

Radicalism, or getting to the root, begins with two propositions: first, history from below or working-class history, and second, the notion that working-class revolution is bound to happen once you gain historical consciousness. I shall try to work out these propositions by considering our building, University Hall. (Investigation puts the rage to work.)

1. University Hall and History from Below
Let us read Bertolt Brecht's poem "A Worker Reads History."

> Who built the seven gates of Thebes?
> The books are filled with names of kings.
> Was it the kings who hauled the craggy blocks of stone?
> And Babylon, so many times destroyed.
> Who built the city up each time?
> In which of Lima's houses,
> That city glittering with gold, lived those who built it?
> In the evening when the Chinese wall was finished
> Where did the masons go?
> Imperial Rome is full of arcs of triumph.
> Who reared them up?
> Over whom did the Caesars triumph?

Byzantium lives in song.
Were all her dwellings palaces?
And even in Atlantis of the legend
The night the seas rushed in,
The drowning men still bellowed for their slaves.

Young Alexander conquered India. He alone?
Caesar beat the Gauls. Was there not even a cook in his army?

Phillip of Spain wept as his fleet was sunk and destroyed.
Were there no other tears?
Frederick the Great triumphed in the Seven Years War.
Who triumphed with him?

Each page a victory
At whose expense the victory ball?
Every ten years a great man,
Who paid the piper?

So many particulars.
So many questions.

Our "particular" is University Hall and our "question" is who hauled its craggy blocks of stone?

The stones which compose our buildings are Wisconsin Lannon stone with Indiana limestone trim. Downstairs in the vestibule a plaque explains that fifty thousand tons of stone make the building. We read in Frank Hickerson's *Tower Builders: The Centennial Story of the University of Toledo* that it was carried in one hundred railway cars.[2] There is not a word about those who quarried the fifty thousand tons or hauled

---

2   Frank Hickerson, *Tower Builders: The Centennial Story of the University of Toledo* (Toledo: University of Toledo Press, 1972), 196–97.

the hundred carloads. The building took four hundred men eleven months to complete in 1931. Who were they? Do we know the name of even one?

The Lannon quarries, a few miles north of Milwaukee, started in the 1830s with pick and crow bar. Lannon stone used to be mainly used for paving and curbs. It is still used for structural backfill, riprap for drainage swales, concrete aggregates, etc. The quarry men were immigrants from Italy and Poland.

Men worked ten-hour days, six-day weeks, at ten cents an hour for unskilled, and two bits to a half dollar for skilled work. They had to pay for their own gloves, however. One store sold gloves. And the work was so rough that they wore out a pair a day. The women scavenged for the used timbers of wood frames which boxed or crated the stone in the railway cars. They needed it for fuel. The communities struggled to obtain garden plots, and permission to keep a pig.[3]

The workers died young of silicosis. They fought back, meeting in the morning at the grindstone to sharpen their tools. The constitution of their union pledged to overthrow capitalism.[4]

Many of Vermont quarrymen were anarchists. Luigi Galleani (1861–1931) worked with the quarrymen of Barre, Vermont. He hid there and published his newspaper advocating direct violent action against tyrants and oppressors. Luigi Galleani believed in propaganda by the deed. His 1905 booklet *La Salute è in voi!* (Health is in you) contained bomb-making instructions.

---

3   Ruth Schmidt, "Lannon and Its Quarries," in *Lannon History: Village of Lannon Golden Jubilee 1930–1980*, ed. Fred Keller (1980).

4   Bernard Sanders, "Vermont Labor Agitator," *Labor History* 15 (March 1974): 261–70. For this and other help I am grateful to two generous scholars of the University of Milwaukee, Dr. Rachel Buff and Professor Michael Gordon.

One of his followers was Mario Buda, who is thought to have exploded a bomb at the Milwaukee police station in 1917, killing nine. Were there Italian anarchists working the Lannon quarries? Among the four hundred men who put the stones on top of each other with such intelligence had some come across Galleani's newspaper, *Cronaca Sovversiva* or "Subversive Chronicle"? At one time there were five thousand subscribers to this newspaper. It is difficult to believe that there were not any subscribers in Lannon or Toledo. Suppose a dozen years after the Milwaukee bombing you're picking and blasting, and wearing out gloves in the Lannon quarry, surely you would have heard about it.

Galleani was deported in 1919 and Mussolini put him in prison back in Italy where he could sing "La Dynamite" all he wanted. He died at the age of seventy in 1931, the year when University Hall, this building, was opened.

Anarchist dynamiters were nothing compared to government or business dynamiters. For instance, take Sir John Fox Burgoyne's classic *A Treatise on the Blasting and Quarrying of Stone* still in print at Galleani's time. He was a British explosives expert, an army engineer who had fought in the Napoleonic Wars, in the Peninsular War (Spain and Portugal), and in New Orleans (1812). In addition to knowledge of America, he directed engineering in Crimea, Ireland, and India. He helped to create an empire by blasting the earth! On page one he writes, reminiscent of Brecht, "The history of the art would oblige us to extend our retrospect to a very early date, to call to mind the structural wonders ... of Thebes." It is doubtful he would know the names of those hauling the craggy blocks of stone.

The general did not wield hand tools unless you consider the swagger stick a tool. The wedge, the mallet, the hammer, the auger, the chisel, and the jumper (that's the big auger to drill the hole to lay the charge before it's tamped).

His knowledge depended on the workers. He quotes one, "Apply your match to which set fire and run as fast as you can."

So the anarchist helps us see that workers make history. Literally they construct the world around us. But not as they please. They have done so through stages of historical development.

2. University Hall and the Niagara Escarpment

Geologically, the rocks of Lannon are the hardest type of limestone. They are called dolostone, or Niagara dolomite. It is very dense, 160 lbs. to the cubic foot. This provides its resistance to abrasion and its compressive strength. It gives to U Hall its durability and distinction.

Lannon stone is part of the great Niagara escarpment. The Genesee River in Rochester, New York, falls three times over this escarpment in raging falls against which the salmon annually run in a furious struggle. The Niagara River flows over it at the famous falls. The escarpment runs north through Ontario on the southern border of Lake Huron, then over northern Michigan, and down the western shore of Lake Michigan on eastern Wisconsin. It is about one thousand miles in length and it was formed some four hundred million years ago.

The dolomite limestone of U Hall was created during the Silurian Period of the Paleozoic Era when a warm shallow sea existed here. Four hundred million years ago the Niagara dolomite was formed from accumulated sediments of the ancient sea. These sediments are made up of calcium and magnesium carbonate which came from the decomposing algae, shells, and skeletons of sea life. The stones of University Hall under the influences of weight, heat, and time were made from earlier life forms, such as brachiopods, cephalopods, crinoids, and corals.

It took about a million years to form the escarpment during the Silurian Period. Indeed it had been the shoreline of a tropical sea during the preceding Ordovician Period. John McPhee tells us what both the industrious and the idle student owe to that Ordovician gunk on the bottom of the shallow waters because it came to form the material of the blackboards of American public schools and the true flatness of the surfaces on the tables in your local pool hall.[5] Study and play!

The Ordovician extinction was the second largest of the five major extinction events in Earth's history in terms of percentage of genera that went extinct and second largest in the overall loss of biota. The cause of extinction appears to have been the movement of Gondwana (the former continent) into the south polar region. This led to global cooling, glaciation, and consequent sea-level fall.

It was a Wisconsin professor, ecologist, farmer, and naturalist, Aldo Leopold, who wrote of the cry of the wolf, "It is an outburst of wild defiant sorrow, and of contempt for all the adversities of the world."[6] If you shoot the wolf to extinction, he showed, then the deer herd grows without limit and soon devours the forest undergrowth. The soil erodes and runs off to the sea, carried miles by rivers which deposit it as silt in the delta. All from the cry of the wolf, his example of the web of life. He called it thinking like a mountain. We call it the trophic cascade.

"There is as yet no ethic dealing with man's relation to land and to the animals and plants which grow upon it." I guess Leopold meant ethics in contrast to economics. The ethics-economics dualism, like the history-nature dualism,

---

5   John McPhee, *The Annals of a Former World* (New York: Farrar, Straus and Giroux, 1999).

6   See *A Sand County Almanac and Sketches Here and There* (New York: Oxford University Press, 1949), 129.

is a relatively recent structure of thought originating with seventeenth-century capitalism.

The Silurian Period was identified by Sir Roderick Murchison, and he named it after a Celtic people of South Wales, the Silures. That was in 1835 about when William Lannon arrived at the place that bears his name in Wisconsin. In 1879 Sir Charles Lapworth identified the Ordovician Period and named it after a Celtic tribe of North Wales, the Ordovices. These Celtic tribes resisted the Roman occupation of the first century of our common era.

3. Stages of History

The narrative of Progress was once also the narrative of Revolution. Marx's stages were primitive communism, ancient slavery, medieval feudalism, then capitalism. The idea that history develops through well-defined, particular stages arose in the eighteenth-century Enlightenment when historians got their stadial notions from the geologists (lithostratification), who in turn learned from the coal miners (back to the workers). Then, as now, it was the fossils of sea creatures found on dry land or high ground that convinced people that the earth once had other configurations of oceans and continents.

The stages of human history had to do with the modes of production, or how the material basis of life was achieved. They were hunting and gathering, domesticated animals, agriculture, and trade and manufactures. In the eighteenth century they had no idea of extinctions. At the time of the French Revolution, Cuvier taught geological catastrophism, to be followed by Lyell and Darwin who taught evolutionism.

Have I failed to describe "the real state of things," which is how Karl Marx defined communism? "Communism is for us not a state of affairs which is to be established, an ideal to which reality [will] have to adjust itself. We call communism the real movement which abolishes the present state of things."[7] It is not pie-in-the-sky. Look around you, Marx is saying. The self-activity of the proletariat will provide you with your answer. You find it in the myriad of contemporary commons whose social contract reads:

> To each according to their needs,
> From each according to their ability.

Marx gave us the base and superstructure. The foundation was laid of technology, work, or economics, then came the family, property, and the state, followed by religion, philosophy, and manners. But language is there throughout, base and superstructure. I hoped to find how the material basis and the ideological superstructure were mutually constituted. Remember, the dictionary is an historical guide to words *and things*. I go to the *Oxford English Dictionary* to understand lexicography, semantics, discourse, philology, linguistics, as though they were tree rings.

To Vico philology was close to etymology, history, speech, and institutions. He had an idea of the "etymologicon." He believed, for example, that "lex," the Latin word for law, had an origin in the early name for acorns back in the hunting and gathering stage, which in the agricultural stage became a cognate for words meaning water and vegetables, and then after the invention of writing, it came to mean words, then with the formation of the state, it came to mean law. Not exactly ontogeny recapitulating phylogeny but certainly etymology recapitulating stadialism.

The revolutionary believes another world is possible. Those without property in the means of subsistence will get us there. That was the thought of Karl Marx. The class has not yet lived up to its world-historical task. How is it going to do this? By trial and error, of course.

---

7   *The German Ideology*, 48.

If Blake wrote truly in the proverbs of hell that "the tigers of wrath are wiser than the horses of instruction," then that truth can be placed in an historical continuum of the tiger's wild, sublime resistance on the one hand and on the other the domestication of animals in the pastoral stage of history. Blake teaches that the stages are coeval. In other words, the trials and errors are there for us to find.

4. Extinction or Revolution?

The Anthropocene is upon us and with it the sixth mass extinction of life.

Various are the definitions. The term suggests a new geological epoch replacing the Holocene, as an epoch in the history of life on earth. Mike Davis says it is characterized as "the emergence of urban-industrial society as a geological force." Zalasiewicz says it signals the human impact on the biological, physical, and chemical processes of the Earth. Its causes include chemical perturbations (carbon, nitrogen), reduxed taxa, species destruction, acidification of oceans, landscape transformation, ozone depletion, etc.[8] The Stratigraphy Commission of the Geological Society of London (founded in 1807) adjudicates geological timescales and is presently considering the "Anthropocene."

"Rage, rage against the dying of the light" wailed Dylan Thomas. The Welsh bard referred to his death, but he might as well have referred to the last extinction dimming the world as dust filled the atmosphere. Twilight at noon.

The Anthropocene is a recent, technical term to refer—so it is proposed—to our geological *epoch*, which is a subdivision of our geological *period*, the Quaternary, which is

---

8   Mike Davis, "Who Will Build the Ark?" *New Left Review* 61 (January–February 2010): 30. Jan Zalasiewicz *et al*, "Stratigraphy of the Anthropocene," *Philosophical Transactions of the Royal Society* 369 (2011): 1050.

a subdivision of our geological *era*, the Cenozoic. These are nesting chronological elements. It makes it possible to compare this extinction with previous ones.

The first great extinction of life occurred at the end of the Ordovician Period and beginning of the Silurian Period, some 445 million years ago. The Ordovician radiation refers to an explosion of marine life forms, 85 percent of which were extinguished, perhaps owing to glaciation caused by the withdrawal of CO_2 from the atmosphere, itself the result of the first land-based life forms, mosses.[9] This "event" transpired in two pulses over a million years!

Capital's science nowadays tells us we are amid a sixth extinction accompanying the Anthropocene. But something is amiss with this, time-wise. The Anthropocene is a chronological category pertaining to the *epoch*, but the first extinction pertains to the *period*. It's like comparing something that takes a few seconds to something that takes a decade or more.

There is a more serious problem. The "Anthropocene" conceals the classes; it takes a species approach.[10] Man or Woman becomes *Homo sapiens*, a species without a history. Why study history at all if it's all just "human nature" or a tale told by an idiot? Same with the term *Humanity*: it hides the foul fiend. These terms reduce history to biology.

There are different classes of people, the working class and the ruling class: the class which rules and the class which is ruled; the class which owns and the class which owns nothing; the class which is rich and the class which is poor. We must approach the classes by history not by a totally external "nature."

9   Elizabeth Kolbert, *The Sixth Extinction: An Unnatural History* (New York: Henry Holt, 2014), chap. 5. My own thinking about the "Anthropocene" and this extinction began with a remarkable discussion at a Retort gathering in Berkeley, California, in 2014.

10 Jason W. Moore, "Anthropocene, Capitalocene & the Myth of Industrialization," three parts, online.

Do not make the mistake of blaming the miners for global warming just because they dig the coal. It is their bosses who send them into the underground. Without bosses, on their own, the Welsh miners loved jazz, they led the fight for universal health care, they fought fascism in Spain, and their choirs were second to none.

When was the "Anthropocene" supposed to have started? Its scientific proponents propose 1800: "We thus suggest that the year AD 1800 could reasonably be chosen as the beginning of the Anthropocene."[11] Even the critic of the concept who prefers "Capitalocene" also finds that 1800 might be an appropriate starting point.

Capital, as an economic system, lines up those who control the means of life against those who do not, accomplishing this division by means of an assortment of instrumentalities that may be summarized as force, money, and bad ideas. The "Capitalocene" is an ugly word which compels us to see the human conflict at the root of historical change. As human agency brought us to this point, it might relieve us of it too, not by the extinction of *homo sapiens* but by the abolition of capitalism. Human agency works through history and that history is one of conflict: Who? whom?

"It is not the light that we need, but the fire; it is not the gentle shower, but thunder. We need the storm, the whirlwind, and the earthquake," said Frederick Douglass as written in powerful graffiti on the walls of the Field House (built also of Lannon stone).

No, I didn't have the time as the deans suggested "to go on the market." Instead I sowed seeds of scholarship up and

---

11   Will Steffen, Jacques Grinevald, Paul Crutzen, and John McNeill, "The Anthropocene: Conceptual and Historical Perspectives," *Philosophical Transactions of the Royal Society* 369 (2011): 849. See also Jan Zalasiewicz et al., "Stratigraphy of the Anthropocene," *ibid.*, 1050.

down as dragon's teeth. I published *The London Hanged*, *The Many-Headed Hydra* (with Marcus Rediker), *The Magna Carta Manifesto*, and *Stop, Thief!* No dean, no provost, no president, no vice-president, no member of the board of trustees ever mentioned them. Colleagues in the history department respected the work and supported it. The first book helped to put capital punishment on the academic agenda. The second helped put the "Atlantic world" on the map. The third, about law and the commons, is still sinking in. Now it is time to revisit revolution. May the dragon's teeth spring up as activists.

It so happens that it is also time for me to revisit my first lecture at the University of Toledo on Edward Despard, a revolutionary, beheaded in 1803. I have been wondering about 1803 for twenty years. Why is it imperative to know what happened in 1803?[12] OK, that was the year Ohio became a state, but I have in mind additional events.

In our era the factory, the prison, the plantation, and patriarchy are the historical institutions of exploitation. They had major boosts in 1803.[13] The expansion of fossil fuel extraction, the thermodynamics of the heat engine, the statutory criminalization of abortion, the expropriation of the agrarian commons, the slaves' victory in Haitian independence, the slaves' defeat in the Louisiana Purchase, the underground of the English craftspeople, the extinction of independent Ireland, and war, War, WAR!

---

12 One of the disciplinary deformations of the historian is a fondness for dates, which in my case has almost reached the stage of an involuntary tic. What delight I felt upon learning that dolomite or the dolostone is named after the French geologist Déodat de Dolomieu, born 1750, died 1801, the year after the Anthropocene commenced and Despard was released from prison! Napoleon appointed him Inspector of Mines.

13 See "The City and the Commons" in *Stop, Thief! The Commons, Enclosures, and Resistance* (Oakland: PM Press, 2014).

We can see the wars as between England representing God, King, and Property and France representing Liberty, Equality, and Fraternity, or we can see them globally as an expansion of capitalist relations, or the introduction of "business as usual" to the Ohio Valley, the Great Lakes, Mexico, Venezuela, India, Afghanistan, Cape Town, etc., etc. It goes back to 1803.

But what about the working class?

Twenty years ago my lecture on the revolutionaries Edward and Catherine Despard saw them not in the exclusive context of the making of the English working class but as Irish and African-American workers as well. I was unable to get in their heads, or to describe the historical experiences that this meant, because my "information about things" was confined to the OED! Language politics destroys the vernacular, it obliterates memory, it extinguishes collective identity.

I omitted the Irish language, I omitted cant, and both are omitted from the OED. I needed therefore an Irish dictionary and a thieves' dictionary. Danny Cassidy supplied the one with a lexicography from below showing how the Irish language, while severely diminished in Ireland, secretly survived in America as slang! The other was actually gathered in 1800–1803 by James Hardy Vaux, an educated thief, in the same prison where Despard had suffered.[14] These two sources help to repair the deficiencies of the OED, and consequently may expand our understanding of class composition at the commencement of the Anthropocene.

One helps us to understand the role of immigrants, especially those with experience against empires, the other provides a light to the underclass or precarious workers,

---

14 Daniel Cassidy, *How the Irish Invented Slang: The Secret Language of the Crossroads* (Petrolia, CA: CounterPunch, 2007), and Noel McLachlan (ed.), *The Memoirs of James Hardy Vaux, Including his Vocabulary of the Flash Language* (London: Heineman, 1964)

especially those experienced in commoning. These are divisions within the working class. According to my U Hall riff the "working class" is that historical power, that force of creation, that hidden factor of economics which when sufficiently gathered unto itself may bring to birth a new society, a new epoch, a new period, and a new era.

Under capitalist control, universities are dying as commons of knowledge, as sites of social regeneration, even as places to read a book. My emotions are clear, even if much thinking and investigation remains to be done. Bitterness availeth us not, it belongs with the stones of the past and their tears. Rage however does not belong there.

I want to indicate biological, chemical, magnetic powers that belong with history. The discussion of the Anthropocene, if nothing else, helps us to see that our metaphors are signs of the times. The cry of the wolf called a previous generation to the web of life. Before that, the abolition of slavery was accompanied by thunder, whirlwind, fire, and earthquake. In 1803 tigers of wrath walked the forest recognizing neither the Stratigraphy Commission of the Geological Society of London nor the Industrial Revolution.

So, to conclude.

Having said my piece, my swan song, I am ready to contribute to this task with the construction workers, the immigrants, the prisoners, the cooks, the nurses, the students, the gardeners, the teachers, and the farmers. Roger Tory Peterson, the birder and inventor of field guides, says that the swan, *Cygnus olor*, does not sing but merely honks, grunts, and occasionally hisses.[15] Aesop, the slave and teller of animal fables, says that the swan, who had been caught by mistake instead of the goose, began to sing as a prelude

15   Roger Tory Peterson, *A Field Guide to Birds* (Boston: Houghton Mifflin, 2001), 49.

to its own demise. His voice was recognized and the song saved his life. Let that be the case with this swan song or swan honk: let the sober vow be recognized again, to unite with the workers of the world. We have the World to gain, the Earth to recuperate. *M'aidez! M'aidez!*

Index

"Passim" (literally "scattered") indicates intermittent discussion of a topic over a cluster of pages.

PM Press is an independent, radical publisher of critically necessary books for our tumultuous times. Our aim is to deliver bold political ideas and vital stories to all walks of life and arm the dreamers to demand the impossible. Founded in 2007 by a small group of people with decades of publishing, media, and organizing experience, we have sold millions of copies of our books, most often one at a time, face to face. We're old enough to know what we're doing and young enough to know what's at stake. Join us to create a better world.

PM Press
PO Box 23912
Oakland CA 94623
510-703-0327
www.pmpress.org

PM Press in Europe
europe@pmpress.org
www.pmpress.org.uk

FRIENDS OF PM

These are indisputably momentous times—the financial system is melting down globally and the Empire is stumbling. Now more than ever there is a vital need for radical ideas.

In the many years since its founding—and on a mere shoestring—PM Press has risen to the formidable challenge of publishing and distributing knowledge and entertainment for the struggles ahead. With hundreds of releases to date, we have published an impressive and stimulating array of literature, art, music, politics, and culture. Using every available medium, we've succeeded in connecting those hungry for ideas and information to those putting them into practice.

Friends of PM allows you to directly help impact, amplify, and revitalize the discourse and actions of radical writers, filmmakers, and artists. It provides us with a stable foundation from which we can build upon our early successes and provides a much-needed subsidy for the materials that can't necessarily pay their own way. You can help make that happen—and receive every new title automatically delivered to your door once a month—by joining as a Friend of PM Press. And, we'll throw in a free T-shirt when you sign up.

Here are your options:
- **$30 a month** Get all books and pamphlets plus 50% discount on all webstore purchases
- **$40 a month** Get all PM Press releases (including CDs and DVDs) plus 50% discount on all webstore purchases
- **$100 a month** Superstar—Everything plus PM merchandise, free downloads, and 50% discount on all webstore purchases

For those who can't afford $30 or more a month, we have **Sustainer Rates** at $15, $10, and $5. Sustainers get a free PM Press T-shirt and a 50% discount on all purchases from our website.

Your Visa or Mastercard will be billed once a month, until you tell us to stop. Or until our efforts succeed in bringing the revolution around. Or the financial meltdown of Capital makes plastic redundant. Whichever comes first.

From SPECTRE from PM Press

Stop, Thief!
The Commons, Enclosures, and Resistance

Peter Linebaugh

ISBN: 978-1-60486-747-3
$21.95   304 pages

In this majestic tour de force, celebrated historian Peter Linebaugh takes aim at the thieves of land, the polluters of the seas, the ravagers of the forests, the despoilers of rivers, and the removers of mountaintops. Scarcely a society has existed on the face of the earth that has not had commoning at its heart. "Neither the state nor the market," say the planetary commoners. These essays kindle the embers of memory to ignite our future commons.

From Thomas Paine to the Luddites, from Karl Marx—who concluded his great study of capitalism with the enclosure of commons—to the practical dreamer William Morris—who made communism into a verb and advocated communizing industry and agriculture—to the 20th-century communist historian E.P. Thompson, Linebaugh brings to life the vital commonist tradition. He traces the red thread from the great revolt of commoners in 1381 to the enclosures of Ireland, and the American commons, where European immigrants who had been expelled from their commons met the immense commons of the native peoples and the underground African-American urban commons. Illuminating these struggles in this indispensable collection, Linebaugh reignites the ancient cry, "STOP, THIEF!"

"There is not a more important historian living today. Period."
—Robin D.G. Kelley, author of *Freedom Dreams: The Black Radical Imagination*

"E.P. Thompson, you may rest now. Linebaugh restores the dignity of the despised luddites with a poetic grace worthy of the master . . . [A] commonist manifesto for the 21st century."
—Mike Davis, author of *Planet of Slums*

"Peter Linebaugh's great act of historical imagination . . . takes the cliché of 'globalization' and makes it live. The local and the global are once again shown to be inseparable—as they are, at present, for the machine-breakers of the new world crisis."
—T.J. Clark, author of *Farewell to an Idea*

From SPECTRE CLASSICS **from PM Press**

William Morris: Romantic to Revolutionary

E.P. Thompson

ISBN: 978-1-60486-243-0
$32.95   880 pages

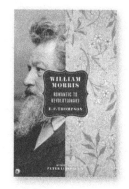

William Morris—the great 19th-century craftsman, architect, designer, poet and writer—remains a monumental figure whose influence resonates powerfully today. As an intellectual (and author of the seminal utopian *News from Nowhere*), his concern with artistic and human values led him to cross what he called the "river of fire" and become a committed socialist—committed not to some theoretical formula but to the day-by-day struggle of working women and men in Britain and to the evolution of his ideas about art, about work and about how life should be lived. Many of his ideas accorded none too well with the reforming tendencies dominant in the labour movement, nor with those of "orthodox" Marxism, which has looked elsewhere for inspiration. Both sides have been inclined to venerate Morris rather than to pay attention to what he said. Originally written less than a decade before his groundbreaking *The Making of the English Working Class*, E.P. Thompson brought to this biography his now trademark historical mastery, passion, wit, and essential sympathy. It remains unsurpassed as the definitive work on this remarkable figure, by the major British historian of the 20th century.

"*Two impressive figures, William Morris as subject and E.P. Thompson as author, are conjoined in this immense biographical-historical-critical study, and both of them have gained in stature since the first edition of the book was published . . . The book that was ignored in 1955 has meanwhile become something of an underground classic—almost impossible to locate in second-hand bookstores, pored over in libraries, required reading for anyone interested in Morris and, increasingly, for anyone interested in one of the most important of contemporary British historians . . . Thompson has the distinguishing characteristic of a great historian: he has transformed the nature of the past, it will never look the same again; and whoever works in the area of his concerns in the future must come to terms with what Thompson has written. So too with his study of William Morris.*"
—Peter Stansky, *The New York Times Book Review*

"*An absorbing biographical study . . . A glittering quarry of marvelous quotes from Morris and others, many taken from heretofore inaccessible or unpublished sources.*"
—Walter Arnold, *Saturday Review*

Printed in the USA
CPSIA information can be obtained
at www.ICGtesting.com
JSHW021956150824
68134JS00055B/1532

9 781629 631073